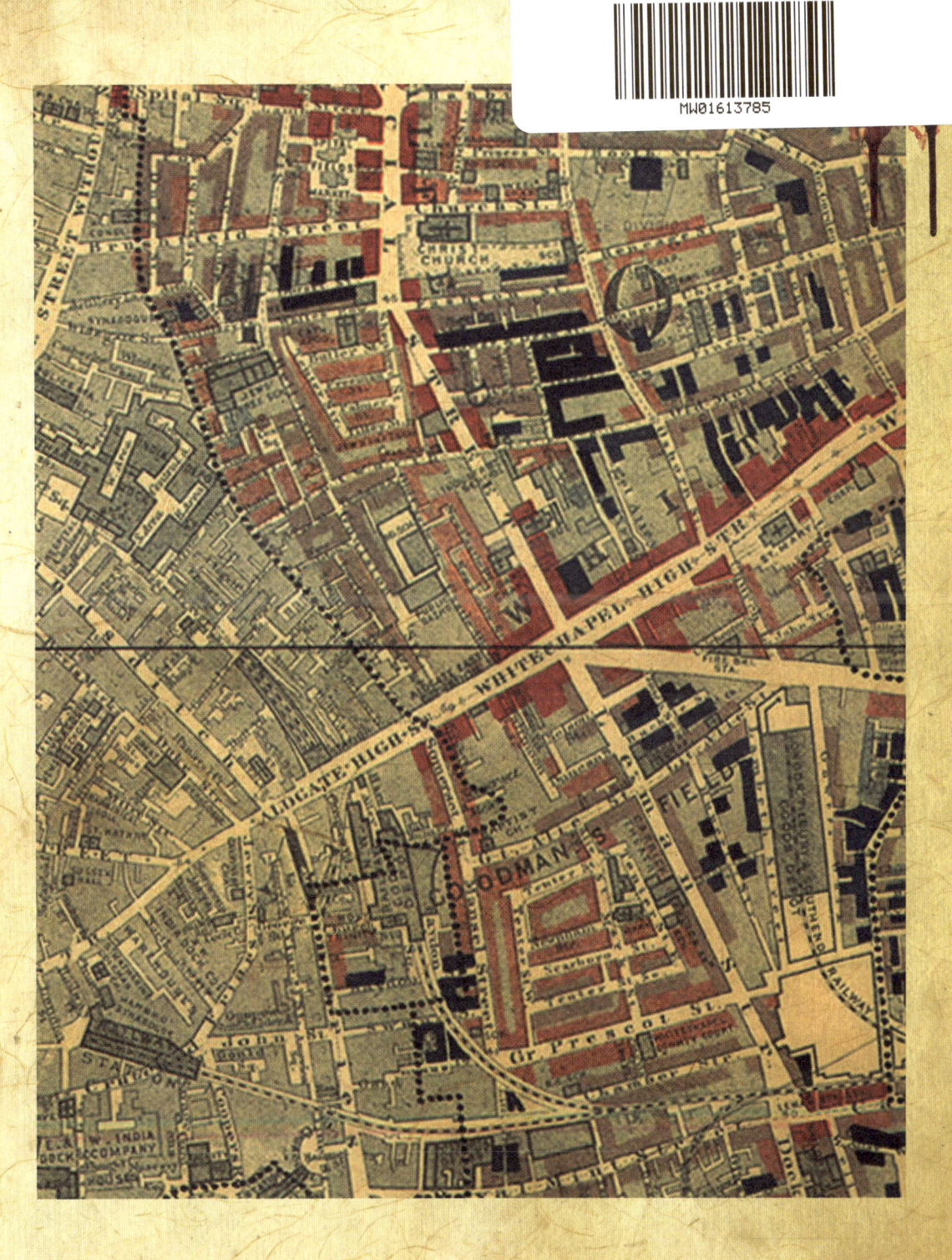

Jack the Ripper

igloobooks

Published in 2016
by Igloo Books Ltd
Cottage Farm
Sywell
NN6 0BJ
www.igloobooks.com

LEO002 0716
2 4 6 8 10 9 7 5 3 1
ISBN 978-1-78557-831-1

Main cover image: © YAY Media AS / Alamy Stock Vector

Cover designed by Nicholas Gage
Edited by Caroline Icke

Written by Geoff Barker

Printed and manufactured in China

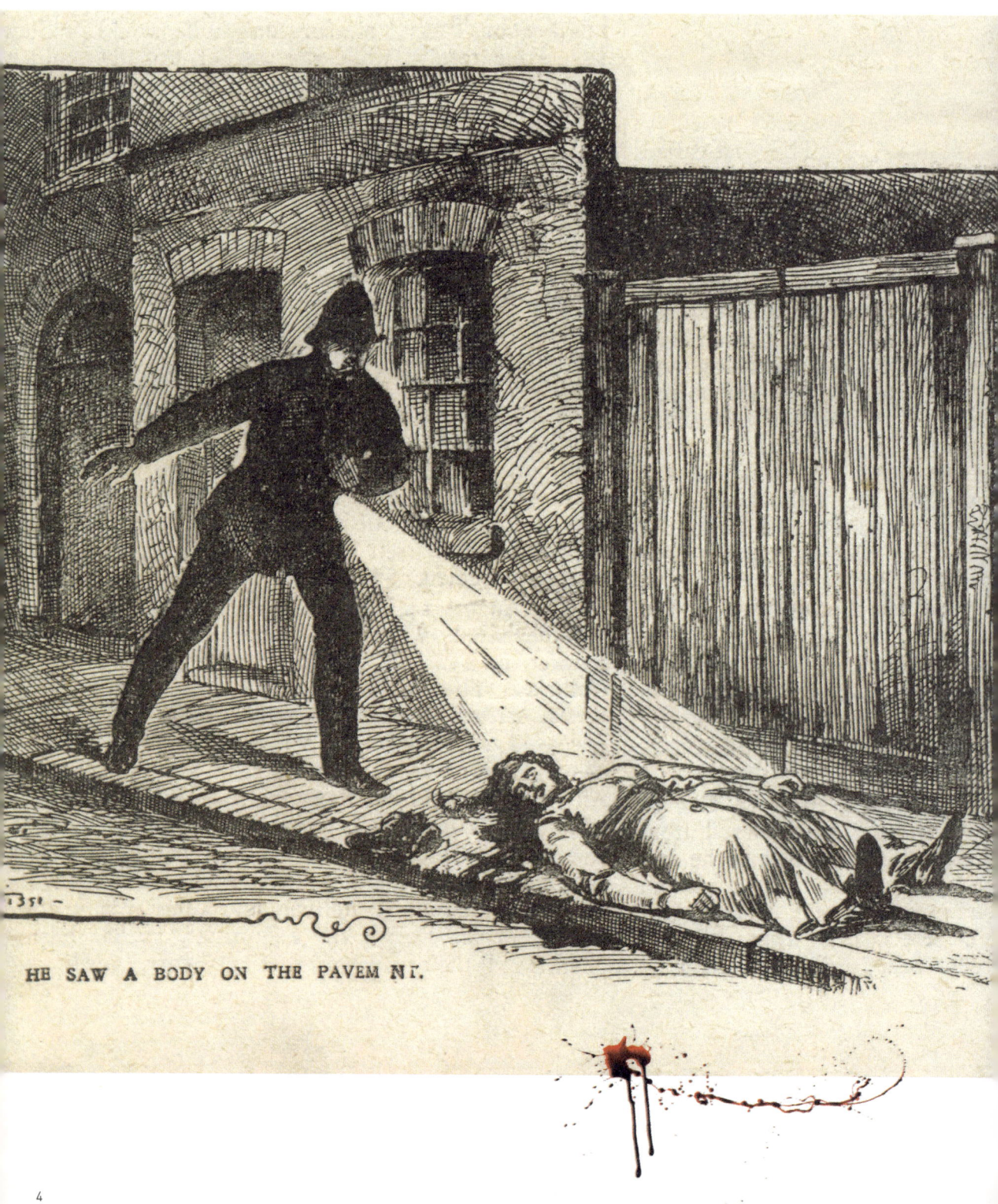

HE SAW A BODY ON THE PAVEMENT.

CONTENTS

Under cover of night, Jack the Ripper would strike in London's dark alleys.

WHO WAS JACK THE RIPPER?

The mere mention of his name conjures up images of seedy Victorian London: cobbled, foggy streets lit by the dim glow of gaslights, prostitutes disappearing into dark alleyways with strangers, and gentlemen wearing top hats slipping into hansom cabs. More than a century has passed since the spate of grisly murders dubbed the "Autumn of Terror", but the story of Jack the Ripper continues to grab the collective imagination. It has become folklore. The difficulty, well over 100 years later, is in separating the truth from the fiction. But that has always been the way with the story of Jack the Ripper – it seems that even in 1888, the fictional element was already overtaking the hard facts of the case.

How much of the stereotypical view of the killer is accurate? In truth, probably very little. In 2006, Jack the Ripper was voted "The Worst Briton Ever" by the British public in a poll carried out by *BBC History Magazine*. The Victorian murderer has become an iconic figure. Many books have been written about him and all sorts of films have been made in recent years. Jack the Ripper was the perfect murderer. He was never caught. His mystery deepens the more it is researched. Attempts to finally close the case by keen Ripperologists, as they are known, appear to be doomed to failure. Theories abound and still we are no closer to knowing his identity.

There is even doubt about the number of women Jack the Ripper killed, but there is no doubt that his murders were those of a very sick and depraved mind. Who was the Ripper? Look at the evidence and the most likely suspects – you decide.

Shown in an 1872 engraving, East End buildings were crammed together.

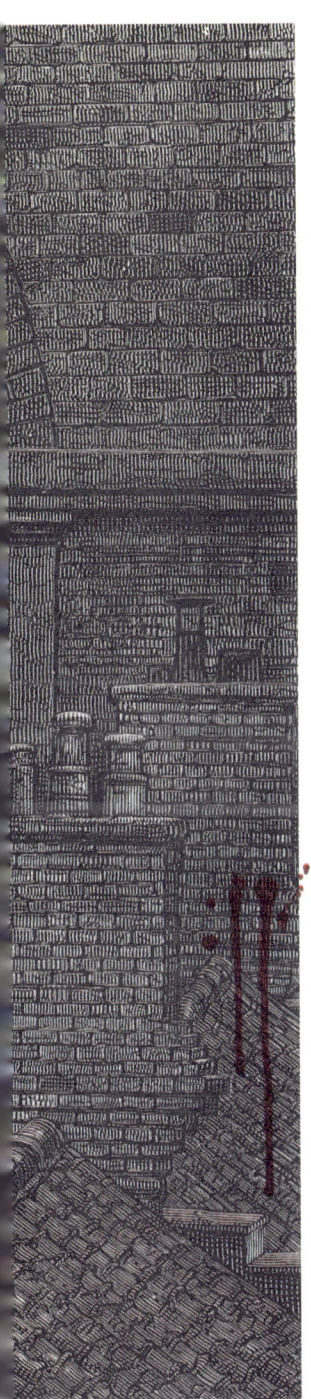

VICTORIAN LONDON

LONDON IN THE 1880s

In the summer of 1887, Queen Victoria celebrated her Golden Jubilee with a lavish banquet for 50 European kings and princes. Although Britain was still a great imperial power, times were changing. Winston Churchill described the 1880s as "the end of an epoch... The great victories had been won... Authority was everywhere broken. Slaves were free. Conscience was free. Trade was free. But hunger and squalor and cold were also free and the people demanded something more than liberty..."

As America and Germany began to compete with Britain in industry, a trade slump led to mass unemployment. The financial powerhouse of the City of London favoured the middle classes, while the poorer districts directly to the east (known as the East End from the 1880s) housed a great underclass, which had to bear the brunt of unemployment.

In his *Tales of Mean Streets* about life towards the end of the 19th century, Arthur Morrison describes the East End of London as "an evil plexus of slums that hide human creeping things". He continues that this "shocking place" is where "filthy men and women live on penn'orths of gin, where collars and clean shirts are decencies unknown, where every citizen wears a black eye and none ever combs his hair."

The poor staged rallies in the years 1886 and 1887 to protest about their awful living conditions, ending in looting from shops and properties in London's West End. Little happened to change the lives of poor East Enders, while the middle and upper classes became more wary and fearful, steering clear of the region.

Whitechapel had some of the worst slums
in London, with people living in squalor.

THE HEART OF DARKNESS

The vicar of St Jude's Church on Commercial Street, the Reverend Samuel Barnett, recognised positive aspects of the East End, describing the "greater part of Whitechapel... as orderly as any part of London". Barnett was a social reformer, aware of the worst parts of the region – the byways to the west and east of Commercial Street, including Dorset Street, Thrawl Street, Wentworth Street and Flower and Dean Street. He referred to this dark heart of East London as "the wicked quarter mile".

Charles Booth, a social reporter, produced a survey of London in 1887, including a "poverty map" which showed where people had to endure the most desperate living conditions – particularly in Whitechapel and Spitalfields. Out of a population of almost half a million East Enders, a third of them were living on or below the poverty line. One in four children would die before reaching the age of five. And half of all men, women and children from the East End – a quarter of a million people in total – were crammed into Whitechapel.

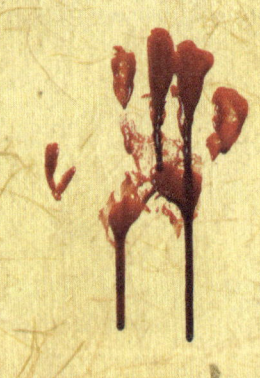

Charles Booth's poverty map marked the poorest areas of the East End in black and dark blue.

Charles Booth (1840–1916)

Many Jewish people fled from persecution in Eastern Europe in the 1880s and made a home in the poor melting-pot of London's East End. Up to 40,000 Jews found terrible cramped living quarters, but they felt safer, far from the barbaric pogroms, or massacres. Many large and extended families had to squeeze themselves into tiny rooms. Common lodging houses offering the most basic of conditions proliferated. It was estimated in 1875 that this type of dilapidated accommodation in Flower and Dean Street held more than 750 people in just over 120 rooms (averaging six people to each tiny room). Many of these dosshouses were little more than health-threatening slums.

In 1888, the East Enders had to face an even greater threat to their grim, impoverished lives. His name was Jack the Ripper.

THE MURDERS

THE WHITECHAPEL MURDERS

In the early morning of 3rd April 1888, Emma Elizabeth Smith was attacked close to her common lodging house in George Street, Spitalfields. She had been walking along Whitechapel Road, having spent a night on the streets soliciting, and was assaulted by three men outside Taylor Brothers Mustard and Cocoa factory in Brick Lane. They robbed her and rammed a blunt instrument into her vagina. The attack was so violent that she had to be helped to nearby London Hospital. After slipping into a coma, she died the following day from peritonitis. The verdict was "wilful murder by some person or persons unknown".

Another prostitute, also living in George Street, perished on 7th August of the same year. Martha Tabram had been stabbed to death 39 times in the stairwell of George Yard Buildings, a wound for every year of her brief life. At her inquest, the coroner described the man committing the murder as a "perfect savage to have attacked the woman in that way". The second Whitechapel murder was to be followed by a series of killings that would be forever associated with Jack the Ripper – and would baffle the combined forces of the Metropolitan and the City of London Police.

Grim murders, starting in August 1888, launched an "Autumn of Terror" in Whitechapel.

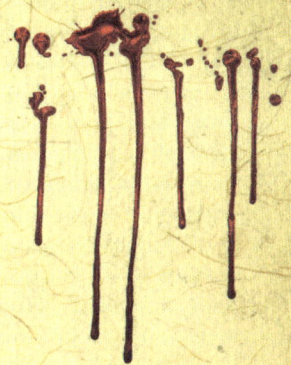

Five further murders came in rapid succession on the mean streets of Whitechapel and Spitalfields. The five, beginning on Friday 31st August 1888 launched an 'Autumn of Terror'. Sir Melville Macnaghten, who served in the Metropolitan Police force from 1889 to 1913, identified these "5 victims & 5 victims only" to be the hand of "the Whitechapel Murderer" in 1894. Brutal murders may have followed and preceded the five victims, but most researchers do not recognise Jack the Ripper as the killer. Now known as the "Canonical Five" (after Ripperologist Martin Fido's phrase), the victims were as follows: Mary Ann Nichols; Annie Chapman; Elizabeth Stride; Catherine Eddowes and Mary Jane Kelly.

CRIME SCENE #1: BUCK'S ROW

At about 3.40am on 31st August 1888, Charles Cross was walking south down Brady Street towards Whitechapel Road. Just before the Roebuck public house, he turned right down a narrow, poorly-lit lane called Buck's Row. He was heading to work as a market porter for Pickford's in Broad Street. Approaching the red-brick building of Essex Wharf, he noticed a bundle in the gutter on the other side of the road, not far from the imposing structure of Buck's Row Boarding School.

The witness later stated that he went to examine the bundle, thinking it was some dumped tarpaulin. Crossing the road, he realised it was the body of a woman lying on her back near a stable yard's gates. As he drew closer to the body, he heard footsteps behind him. Robert Paul, another market porter, was also making his way along Buck's Row to go to work at Corbett's Court, and he joined Cross by the lifeless woman, whose skirts were raised up to her waist. Paul felt for a heartbeat, saying "I think she's breathing, but it's very little, if she is." Both realised she was very close to death, and left her, continuing together west along Buck's Row into White's Row to alert the authorities. They soon found Police Constable Mizen at the junction of Hanbury Street and Baker's Row (today's Vallance Road) and told him of their awful discovery.

Meanwhile, PC John Neil from J Division (Bethnal Green) was patrolling his beat – circling a small area along Whitechapel Road between Baker's Row to the west and Brady Street to the east. He emerged from Thomas Street into White's Row and continued his way east along Buck's Row, but without meeting witnesses Cross and Paul. After passing the Boarding School, he discovered the body of Mary Ann Nichols. PC Neil saw blood draining from her neck, where her throat had been slit. Another officer, PC Thain, soon joined Neil, who asked him to fetch a doctor. But it was too late. Mary Ann Nichols, the first victim of Jack the Ripper, was dead.

Thought by many to be the Ripper's first victim,
Mary Ann Nichols was murdered in Buck's Row.

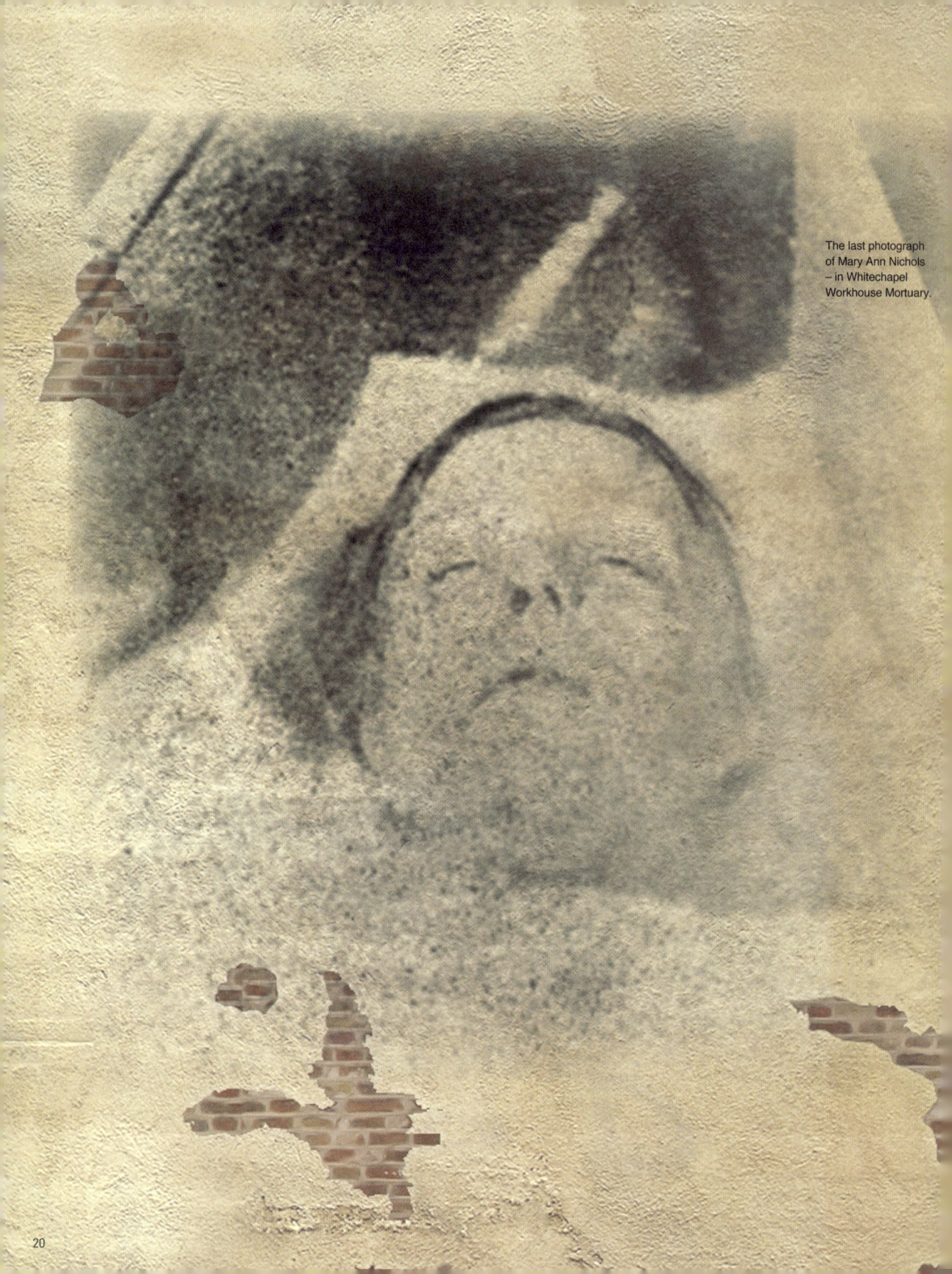

The last photograph of Mary Ann Nichols – in Whitechapel Workhouse Mortuary.

POST-MORTEM OF THE FIRST VICTIM

Summoned by PC Thain from his surgery at 152 Whitechapel Road, Dr. Rees Llewellyn arrived soon afterwards at the scene of the crime. He made a cursory examination of the body and confirmed that the woman was dead and had died only half an hour before. He believed that she had been killed on the spot. Llewellyn made a further lengthy examination of the body at the mortuary shed at Old Montague Street Workhouse Infirmary the following morning.

Dr. Llewellyn's post-mortem discovered small bruises to both sides of the jaw, probably caused by the recent pressure of a thumb and finger – suggesting that the killer had held the woman's throat, prior to slitting it twice. Both cuts were deep, severing the large arteries of the neck. The first cut was about 4 inches (10 cm) long. The second incision was about 8 inches (20 cm) in length, stretching from ear to ear, and both cuts went right down through to the vertebrae.

The same instrument, probably a strong-bladed knife, had been used to make a deep, hacking gash into the left side of the lower part of the abdomen and as far up as the sternum (or breastbone), so that the intestines were exposed. There were similar cuts on the right side, as well as further slashes across the abdomen. None of the internal organs were removed from the body by the murderer.

From the visible injuries and mutilations, Dr. Llewellyn believed that the killer was left handed, attacking the victim from the front. The doctor later expressed doubts about his original assumptions, as the throat wounds could have been consistent with a right-handed killer attacking the victim from behind. He concluded that the murderer must have had "some rough anatomical knowledge". He also believed that the wounds, taking a mere four or five minutes to inflict, suggested that this was the work of a single killer.

THE INQUEST

Dr. Rees Llewellyn (second left), who examined the body, was present at Nichols' inquest.

SKETCHES AT THE INQUEST

The identity of the unfortunate victim was not clear at first. Her sole possessions were a comb, pocket handkerchief, broken mirror and a little black straw bonnet found next to her corpse. Eventually, she was recognised as a woman living at 18 Thrawl Street. Ellen Holland, an occupant of the same lodging house knew her simply as 'Polly'. The victim's petticoats showed a laundry mark of Lambeth Workhouse, and an inmate of the workhouse called Mary Ann Monk identified the deceased as Mary Ann Nichols. The victim's estranged husband, William Nichols, subsequently identified the body, saying "Seeing you as you are now, I forgive you for what you have done to me."

Whitechapel Working Lads' Institute (next to the present Whitechapel Underground station) was the scene of the inquest of Mary Ann Nichols, opening on 1st September 1888. The coroner for the South-Eastern Division of Middlesex, a flamboyant character named Wynne Edward Baxter, criticised the police for not seeing the mutilations to Nichols' abdomen before her body was removed for examination. He also condemned the lack of adequate facilities at the mortuary. Nichols was buried at Ilford cemetery on 6th September 1888, but her inquest was adjourned a number of times until it finally closed towards the end of September.

With such a high-profile case on their hands, the police wanted to solve the brutal murder of Mary Ann Nichols quickly. It was also the third recent murder in the area. Although it had taken place on J Division's territory, H Division constable PC Mizen had reported it, so they, too, had an interest in the case. Inspector Abberline was moved from Scotland Yard back to Whitechapel to organise the work of the detectives.

The press fuelled interest in a man known as 'Leather Apron', who extorted money from prostitutes, and many fearful locals believed he was the Whitechapel Murderer. Leather Apron was identified as John Pizer by the police, who then downplayed his role as a suspect. Whoever the true killer was, just over a week after the Nichols' murder, he had struck once more.

OUTCASTS SLEEPING IN SHEDS IN WHITECHAPEL.

The *Illustrated London News* showed prostitutes sleeping
in the streets at the time of the Whitechapel murders.

WALKING THE STREETS

Habitually linked with poverty, prostitution in Victorian London was regarded by many as 'the great social evil'. However, the social problem was a complex issue and not all Victorians shared the view that prostitution was chosen by many women out of economic necessity. Sex provided a welcome escape from harsh reality for the poor 'unfortunates' (as prostitutes were known at the time), and it also gave them an income. One contemporary social commentator asked, "Who can wonder that young girls wander off into a life of immorality, which promises release from such conditions?"

Unemployment was becoming a problem, but many resourceful people managed to cope. In the 1880s they would need to find fourpence a day for a bed and a further threepence to eat. There were jobs, but many of them were undesirable ways to earn a living: you could be a 'pure-finder' and collect dog excrement off the streets for the tanning trade; if you had the heart for it and a strong nose, as a sewer-hunter, you could earn more than two pounds a week. Women from the slums of the East End could earn more turning tricks as a prostitute in one night than slogging away long hours in a sweatshop for a week. It is little wonder that many turned to prostitution.

Many women sold their bodies regularly, while others solicited on a more casual basis, for example if their families needed a supplementary income. Police estimated that there were about 1200 prostitutes in the infamous 'wicked quarter mile' of Whitechapel, most of them 'of a very low condition'.

Well-meaning Victorians wanted to purge the East End of its worst sins, and about 200 brothels were forced to close in the late 1880s. Prostitutes were forced to move away or go out and find their clients on the streets. It was very bad timing. The 'unfortunates' became much easier prey for Jack the Ripper.

THE LIFE OF MARY ANN NICHOLS

Aged 43 at her death, Mary Ann Nichols was the first official victim of Jack the Ripper. She was born in August 1845, the daughter of locksmith Edward Walker of Dean Street, Fetter Lane, London. Known by many as 'Polly', she was quite short at 5 feet, 2 inches (1.57 m) with grey eyes and greying hair. She had a scar on her forehead from a childhood accident and was also missing her front teeth from a fight.

Polly married William Nichols, a Fleet Street printer, when she was 19. There are records of them living together for six years (c.1874–1880) at Peabody Buildings in Stamford Street. During this time they had five children. William briefly had an affair with the midwife of their fourth child, Eliza Sarah in 1877. After years of arguments, said to be exacerbated by Polly's drinking problem, the couple finally separated in 1880. William Nichols looked after the children except the eldest, Edward John, who moved to his grandfather's house. Mary Ann Nichols entered Lambeth Workhouse, where she received an allowance of five shillings a week for two years from her husband. He discontinued the payments in 1882, when he discovered that she was living as a prostitute.

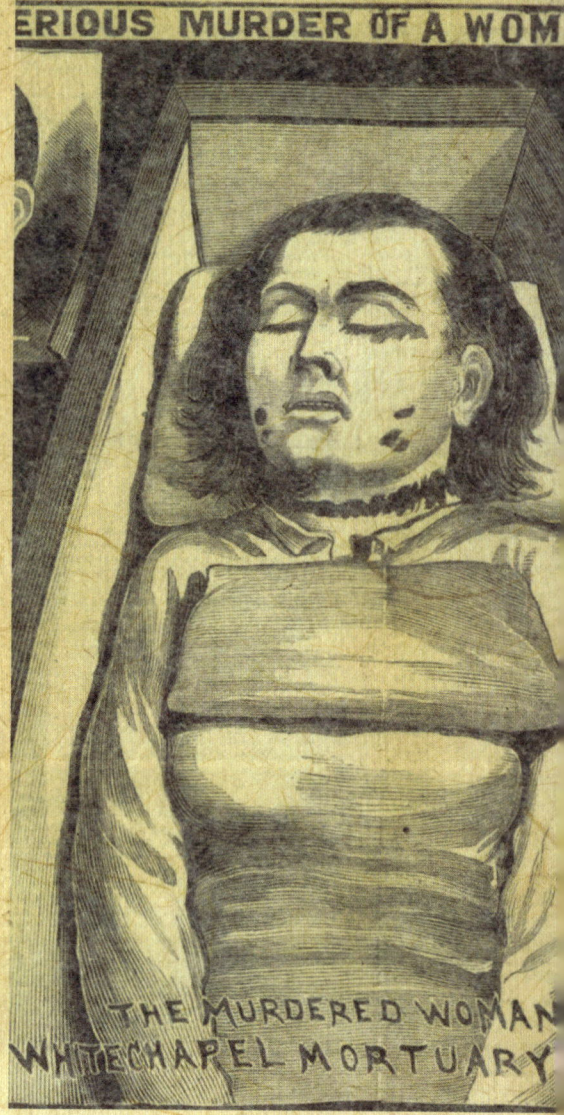

How the *Illustrated Police News* reported the murder on 8th September 1888.

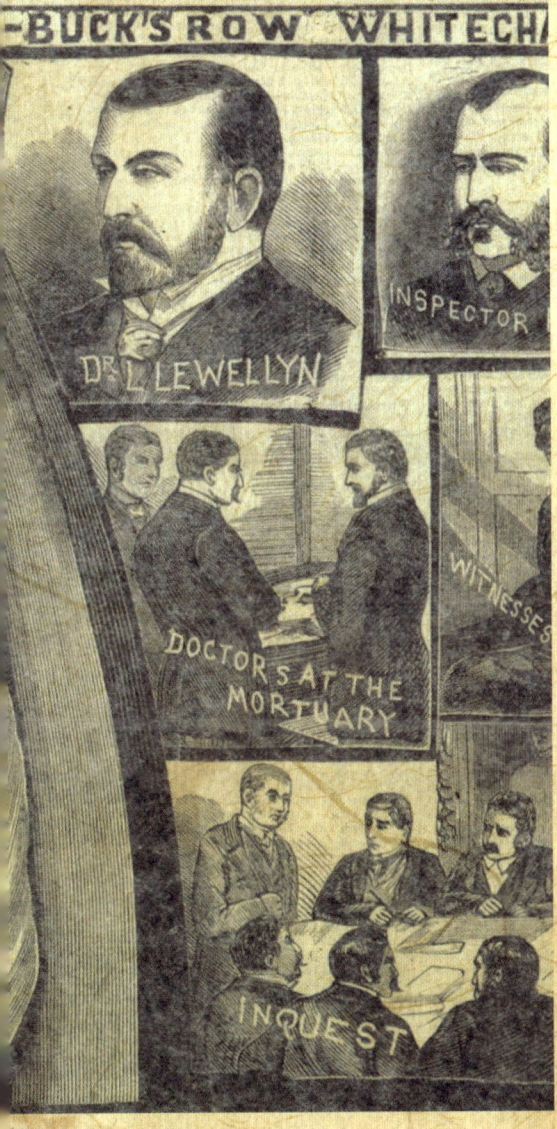

Records show that she lived in a variety of workhouses until August 1888. At the beginning of the month, she moved to a common lodging house called Wilmott's at 18 Thrawl Street, where she shared a room with three other women and a bed with Ellen Holland. Three weeks later, on 24th August 1888, she stayed at the notorious 'White House' at 56 Flower and Dean Street. This was a dosshouse which allowed men and women to sleep together. Her move to this house of ill-repute was a brief one, because the Whitechapel Murderer cut her life short on the last day of August 1888.

THE LAST HOURS OF MARY ANN NICHOLS

Inspector Joseph Helson reported that Mary Ann Nichols was seen leaving the Frying Pan public house on the corner of Brick Lane and Thrawl Street at about 12.30am on 31st August 1888. Her old lodging room at Wilmott's was just down the road at number 18 Thrawl Street. She popped in at about 1.30am and was spotted by the lodging-house deputy sitting next to the fire in the kitchen. He demanded fourpence for a bed for the night, which she did not have. The deputy reminded her that, having stayed at Wilmott's earlier in the month, she knew the rules of the house and would have to leave.

One contemporary newspaper reported that, appearing inebriated, she showed little concern and stated boldly; "I'll soon get my doss money. See what a jolly bonnet I've got now." No-one had seen her bonnet before, but it was the same hat found by Nichols' body in Buck's Row a little over two hours later.

It appears that Mary Ann Nichols walked back along Thrawl Street, and may have returned to the Frying Pan pub on the corner of the street. The next sighting of her was at 2.30am – about an hour before her death – on Osborn Street, the road south of Brick Lane. Mary Ann Nichols' friend, Ellen Holland, met her former Thrawl Street lodger and bed-mate on the corner of Osborn Street and Whitechapel Road. Ellen recalled seeing her friend staggering, quite drunk, then slumping against a wall. She tried to persuade Mary Ann to return with her to Wilmott's for the night, but Nichols was insistent that she would soon earn the fourpence she required from a willing punter. She probably headed east along the main thoroughfare of Whitechapel Road, before she met a stranger on the dark, cobbled byway of Buck's Row. By 3.40am Mary Ann Nichols was dead.

Prostitutes would meet their clients in the street, then search for a dark alleyway.

The body of the second victim was found between the steps and the fence.

CRIME SCENE #2:
29 HANBURY STREET

Twenty-nine Hanbury Street was a plain brick-built three-storey house in Spitalfields. The ground floor had a shop front and in 1888, above the door was the sign 'Mrs. A Richardson – Packing Case Maker'. Inside the front door, a narrow passage led from the hallway the length of the building to the rear of the house. From a back door without a lock, there were two stone steps into a dingy yard with an outside lavatory and a shed. The yard of number 29 was separated from neighbouring properties by old fences. There was no exit at the rear.

Mrs. Amelia Richardson was a widow who had taken over her husband's packing-case business. She rented the whole house and sub-let the rooms to hardworking tenants. John Davis, a 56-year-old market porter at Leadenhall Market lived on the third floor in a room at the front of the house, along with his wife and three adult sons. On Friday 7th September 1888, Davis had gone to bed early, at around 8.00pm. He had a restless night, hearing the nearby bells of Christ Church ring at 5.45am early on the Saturday morning.

Davis rose from his bed, made a cup of tea in his room and headed downstairs. The door at the front of the house was wide open. The back door was closed. Davis pushed the rear door open and between the stone steps and the fence he saw the body of a woman, slashed with the most appalling mutilations.

John Davis ran back through the house and rushed into the street for help. He found three men to witness a scene they would never forget. The woman's abdomen had been ripped open – her intestines were severed from the abdominal wall, and strung over her shoulder. Davis said, "It was part of her body. I did not examine the woman, I was too frightened at the dreadful sight."

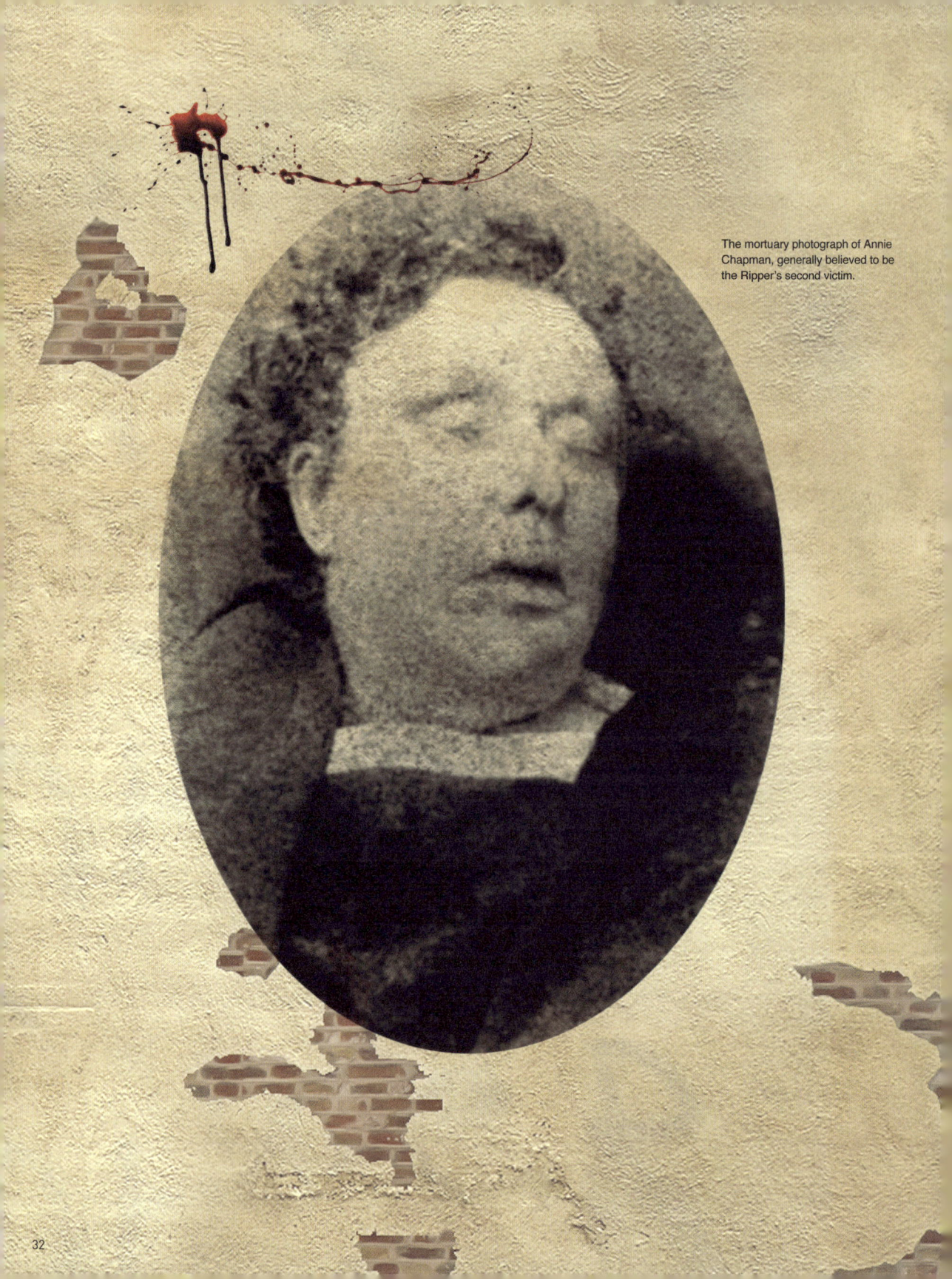

The mortuary photograph of Annie Chapman, generally believed to be the Ripper's second victim.

POST-MORTEM OF THE SECOND VICTIM

Arriving at the scene of the crime at around 6.30am, Dr. George Bagster Phillips, the police surgeon for H Division, viewed the corpse. The legs of the victim were drawn up, with the knees turned outwards. The left arm was placed across the breast and the neck was cut deeply, with smears of blood on the nearby fence and a pool of blood on the ground from the slit throat. The killer had cut through the abdomen and severed the intestines, arranging them over the victim's right shoulder and on the ground at the crime scene, while part of the stomach lay close to the left shoulder. Dr. Phillips, along with Inspector Joseph Chandler, searched the back yard for clues. Some personal items, including a piece of muslin and two combs, were at the feet of the victim.

Dr. Phillips performed the post-mortem examination at the Whitechapel mortuary on the 8th September. He observed bruising on the top of the victim's chest and face, suggesting the killer had held the victim, Annie Chapman, by the lower jaw as he cut her throat. He believed that the murderer had strangled or suffocated Chapman to death before he made a long, deep incision into her throat. The deceased was wearing a neckerchief.

The murderer had removed the uterus, upper part of the vagina and a large portion of the bladder from the body – and taken them from the site of the murder. From his examinations, Dr. Phillips believed that the weapon used to kill would have been a sharp narrow blade at least 6.5 inches (17 cm) long. He also thought that the killer had some anatomical knowledge; the mutilations would have taken at least 15 minutes. He also estimated that if the killer had carried them out with care, they would have taken up to an hour to perform.

THE INQUEST

The inquest was held at the Working Lads' Institute in Whitechapel two days after the post-mortem. Dr. Phillips decided not to give a complete report because he considered that some of the grisly details of the murder would be too horrific for the jury and the public. Dr. Phillips estimated that the time of death was roughly 4.20am, which cast into doubt the timings of a number of reported sightings and eyewitness accounts.

Albert Cadosch, who lived at number 27 Hanbury Street, stepped outside into his back yard between 5.20 and 5.30am on Saturday 8th September. He overheard a couple talking in the yard of number 29 next door. He heard a woman say "No", then a few minutes later there was a scuffle. Something, or perhaps someone, fell against the fence. He did not suspect that anything was amiss though, so he headed off to work. As he passed Christ Church in Spitalfields, he noticed the clock reading 5.32am.

At approximately 5.30am, Elizabeth Long was walking down Hanbury Street. She observed a couple talking on the pavement and identified the woman as the deceased, Annie Chapman. Long described the man as not much taller than Annie Chapman and about 40 years of age. Wearing a deerstalker hat, he had a dark complexion and a "shabby genteel appearance". She heard the man ask Annie, "Will you?" to which she replied, "Yes." Elizabeth Long stated that the man sounded and appeared like a foreigner.

Based on Dr. Phillips findings, the coroner Edwin Wynne Baxter concluded that Cadosch's estimation of the time was incorrect. Similarly, Mrs. Long's observations were also doubted because of the time discrepancies. However, it is possible that Dr. Phillips' estimation of the time of death was too early. Baxter closed the inquest on the 26th September, concluding that the killer had sound anatomical knowledge – more than that of someone who worked in a slaughterhouse.

Christ Church, Spitalfields, was
built in the early 18th century.

THE LIFE OF ANNIE CHAPMAN

Born Eliza Anne Smith in Paddington in 1841, Annie Chapman was the second victim of Jack the Ripper. Her father, George Smith, was a lifeguardsman, married to Ruth Chapman. Annie married another Chapman, called John, in 1869 and together they had three children. Emily Ruth died in 1882 of meningitis and Annie's disabled son John had to move to a 'cripple's home'.

Annie appears to have abandoned her family in Windsor shortly before her daughter Emily's death, when she moved to London. She received a weekly allowance of 10 shillings from her husband until his death in 1886. Annie would have struggled to survive after the loss of this regular income and she sold her own crochet work, as well as matches and flowers to support herself. For a time she lived with a sieve maker, known as Jack Sivvey. However, from about May 1888, Annie Chapman lived mainly at number 35 Dorset Street, at Crossingham's lodging house. Although there are some reports of alcoholism, it seems that at the time of her death, she had managed to curb her drinking.

Annie Chapman, shown in life and in death, in the *Illustrated Police News* (22nd September 1888).

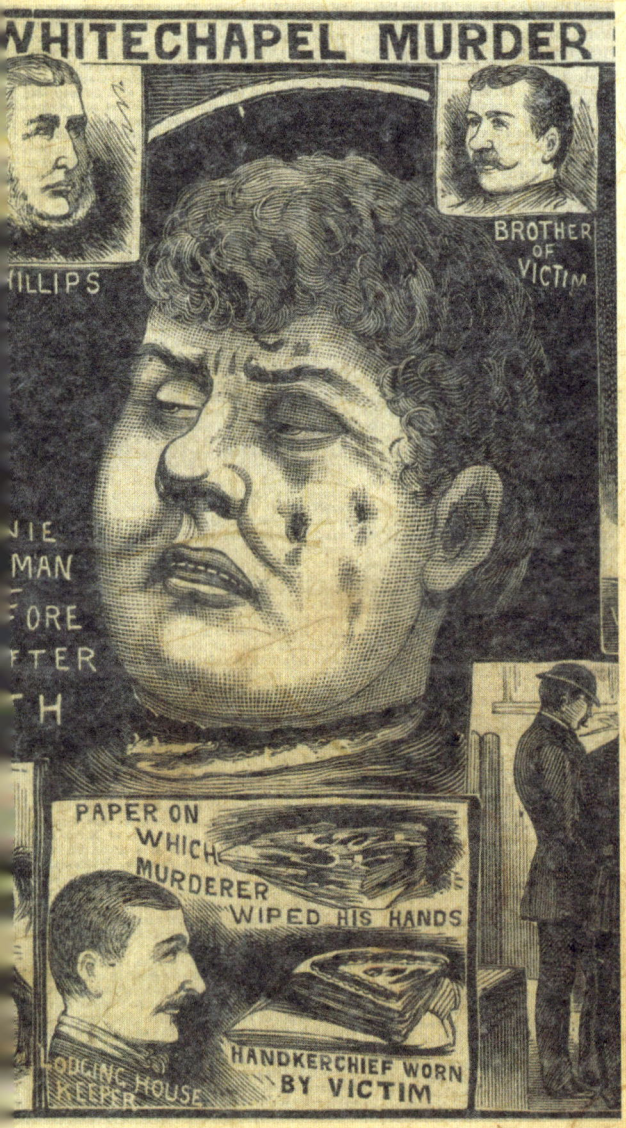

'Dark Annie', as she was known to many, was quite short and plump, at only 5 feet (1.52 m) tall, with dark brown wavy hair. She had blue eyes and a fair complexion, with perfect front teeth. Having examined her corpse at the post-mortem, Dr. Phillips stated that Annie Chapman was undernourished and that chronic diseases of the lungs and brain membranes would have been likely to have led to an early death. Tragically, her life was cut even shorter and her body unceremoniously splayed out in a grubby back yard in Spitalfields.

THE LAST HOURS OF ANNIE CHAPMAN

Suffering a black eye, Annie Chapman had a fight with a woman called Eliza Cooper on the night of Saturday 1st September 1888 at the Britannia pub, on the corner of Dorset Street. She went on to spend the night down the road at 35 Dorset Street with Ted Stanley at Crossingham's lodging house. On Wednesday the 5th September, feeling unwell, she went to the local casual ward (for the 'casual poor') which was part of the workhouse, where conditions were atrocious. She stayed there until Friday, when she returned with some medicine. Annie saw her friend Amelia Palmer at around 5.00pm, telling her that she was still sick, but needed to pull herself together – and earn enough money to find a bed for the night.

On the day of Annie's death, at shortly after 1.30am on Saturday the 8th September, John Evans the nightwatchman at Crossingham's demanded fourpence from Annie to stay the night at the lodging house. She replied that she would get it and went to the office of the deputy, Timothy Donovan, to ask him to save a bed for her that night. Evans walked Annie to the front door to make sure she left the building. He may have been the last person who saw her alive – he thought she was drunk as she headed up Little Paternoster Row towards Brushfield Street.

According to the testimony of Elizabeth Long – having identified the body of the victim in the mortuary – she saw Annie Chapman talking to a gentleman on the pavement of Hanbury Street. She heard their conversation, which could be taken as Annie agreeing to go somewhere with the man. If Elizabeth Long heard correctly, and this was indeed Annie, then the destination was probably the back yard of number 29 Hanbury Street.

Contemporary sketches reconstructed the
victim's last movements on 8th September 1888.

Punch cartoon *Nemesis of Neglect* showed
how crime flourished in awful social conditions.

JACK THE SOCIAL REFORMER

With the horrific death of Annie Chapman on 8th September 1888, the British press had plenty to report. One week afterwards, The *East London Observer* concentrated on East London streets, with an "appearance of mingled excitement, awe and indignation" and the crowd's "desire for vengeance." The article continues in a sensational vein; "the latest butchery of Annie Chapman at Hanbury Street has driven the inhabitants of Whitechapel nearly crazy."

However, it should be remembered that these were exceptional times, with ordinary people driven by adrenaline and pure fear. Meanwhile, the *Daily Telegraph* looked at the need for change in the poorest districts: "Dark Annie's dreadful end has compelled a hundred thousand Londoners to reflect what it must be like to have no home at all except the 'common kitchen' of a low lodging house... to be turned out after midnight to earn the requisite pence, anywhere and anyhow; and in course of earning it to come across your murderer and to caress your assassin."

Social reform was in the air. Sidney Godolphin Osborne wrote a letter to the *Times*, published on the 18th September, comparing the luxuries of London palaces and mansions with the East End's "warren of foul alleys" and their "atmosphere of godless brutality". The Whitechapel Murderer was seen by some as an almost inevitable product of the area.

Writing to the *Star*, George Bernard Shaw suggested ironically that the unknown killer was a social reformer; "Whilst we conventional Social Democrats were wasting our time on education, agitation and organisation, some independent genius has taken the matter in hand, and by simply murdering and disembowelling four women, converted the proprietary press to an inept sort of communism." The killings, though horrific, had focused attention on the larger social problem of the dire living conditions in much of the East End.

CRIME SCENE #3: DUTFIELD'S YARD

Dutfield's Yard was a small cobbled area between numbers 40 and 42 Berner Street, running south from Commercial Road. The third victim of Jack the Ripper was found in the narrow passage between the two brick buildings at 1.00am on 30th September 1888. Number 40 Berner Street was a meeting-place for a group of radicals, social democrats and anarchists, known as the International Working Men's Education Club.

Having sold cheap jewellery at the market at Westow Hill near Crystal Palace, the steward of the Club, a Russian Jew named Louis Diemschutz, was returning to East London by pony and cart very late on the Saturday night of 29th September 1888. He lived on the Berner Street premises of the club with his wife and it was his custom to return home after midnight on a Saturday. He passed a tobacconist near home, noting that it was 1.00am on the Sunday morning. He intended to drop off some goods at Dutfield's Yard, before taking his pony to its stables in George Yard. He passed through the open gates to the side of the club, but his pony was reluctant to enter the yard and shied away.

In the dark, Diemschutz saw a bundle on the ground. He prodded it with the handle of his whip, then got down from his cart. He lit a match and realised it was the body of a woman, either drunk or dead. He rushed into the passage to find his wife in the front room on the ground floor, with other club members. Diemschutz returned to the body with a candle, accompanied by Isaac Kozebrodsky and others. They could see blood trickling away from the lifeless body – her throat was cut and her hands and wrists were also covered in blood.

Looking into Dutfield's Yard, "X" marks the spot of the murder.

The mortuary photograph of third victim, Elizabeth Stride.

POST-MORTEM OF THE THIRD VICTIM

At 4.30am on 30th September 1888, the dead body of Elizabeth Stride was removed to the mortuary in the grounds of the church of St George-in-the-East. It was not clear who the deceased was, and in fact, for some time – after the false identification at the mortuary by a woman named Mary Malcolm – the police were none the wiser.

The immediate priority was to examine the corpse. The post-mortem began at 3.00pm on the 1st October, with both Dr. George Bagster Phillips and Dr. Blackwell present. They found a long, clean incision in the victim's throat, running from left to right, and about 6 inches (15 cm) in length. It began about 1 inch (2 cm) below the angle of the jaw and ended on the other side of the neck, slightly lower below the angle of the right jaw. The gash had almost cut the windpipe in half.

It appears that the victim would have bled to death fairly slowly, unable to make a sound to raise the alarm. Unlike with earlier victims of the Ripper, they found no other cuts.

The doctors discovered pressure marks over both of the present victim's shoulders, under the clavicles (collar bones) and on the chest. This bruising was consistent with two hands grabbing the shoulders and pressing down forcibly. They believed the throat was cut either while Stride was falling to the ground, or lying on the cobbles – blood would have spurted if she had been standing upright. The killer had been to the right of the victim when he cut her throat, left to right. The examining doctors agreed that the cause of death was clear – the left carotid artery was severed and windpipe divided, resulting in haemorrhage.

THE LIFE OF ELIZABETH STRIDE

Elizabeth Stride, the third victim of Jack the Ripper, was born on 27th November 1843, in a small rural parish to the north of Gothenburg, Sweden. Named Elisabeth Gustafsdotter, she was the second of four children to Gustaf Ericsson, a farmer and his wife Beatta. On 21st April 1865, Elizabeth gave birth to a still-born girl, and making a career as a prostitute in Gothenburg, was treated twice for venereal diseases. The following year, Elizabeth moved to London, marrying carpenter John Stride on 7th March 1869, who died in October 1884 of heart disease.

At the time of her death, 'Long Liz' was 44 years of age and 5 feet, 2 inches (1.57 m) tall. She had dark brown curly hair, grey eyes and her upper front teeth were missing. These facts are true, but some of her life story is more hazy. It appears that Elizabeth Stride liked to tell a tale how she, along with her husband and children, were aboard the ill-fated paddle steamer the *Princess Alice*, when it struck the *Bywell Castle*, a large coal vessel on the River Thames. The tragedy took place on 3rd September 1878, when more than 600 passengers on board the steamer died. The disaster was tragically real, but Stride's story was a fiction. She and her husband had no children together, and there were no records of the name Stride in the register of deaths.

From 1885, Elizabeth Stride lived with a waterside labourer named Michael Kidney for about three years. They both liked to drink heavily, leading to an increasingly chaotic lifestyle, including at least seven drunk and disorderly charges against Stride at Thames Magistrates Courts during 1887 and 1888. She split up from Kidney on 25th September, taking up lodgings at her preferred dosshouse at 32 Flower and Dean Street.

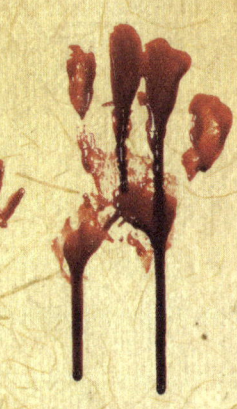

A sketch of Elizabeth Stride in the *Illustrated Police News*.

THE LAST HOURS OF ELIZABETH STRIDE

At about 11.45pm on Saturday 29th September 1888, a labourer called William Marshall was standing in the doorway of his house at number 64 Berner Street. He saw a man and woman a few doors away on the other side of the street – he later identified the corpse of Stride as the woman he had seen. They kissed openly in the street, which Marshall found unusual, because the man was decently dressed, wearing a black coat and a small peaked cap "something like a sailor would wear". He overheard the man say, "You would say anything but your prayers." The couple headed away up the street towards the crossroads at Fairclough Street, in the direction of Dutfield's Yard.

At about 12.30am during his beat, H Division's PC William Smith saw a couple in Berner Street, on the opposite side of the road to Dutfield's Yard. He recalled that the man was about 28 years old, 5 feet, 7 inches (1.70 m) tall with a respectable air, wearing a dark coat and a hard felt deerstalker hat. He was carrying a package about 18 inches (45 cm) long and 6 inches (15 cm) wide, which was wrapped in newspaper. PC Smith saw nothing suspicious and continued north along Berner Street towards Commercial Road.

A quarter of an hour later, a dock labourer James Brown was making his way back home from a shop when he saw a couple on Fairclough Street. The woman had her back against the wall to the boarding school (on the corner of Fairclough and Berner Street), while the man had his arm propped against the wall behind her. Brown overheard the woman say, "No, not tonight... some other night." He believed the woman was Elizabeth Stride and that the man was around 5 feet, 7 inches (1.70 m) tall, and wearing a hat. The timing and reliability of Brown's sighting at 12.45am on the morning of 30th September 1888, however, may be thrown into doubt by a witness named Israel Schwartz.

An artist's impression depicts the murder of Elizabeth Stride.

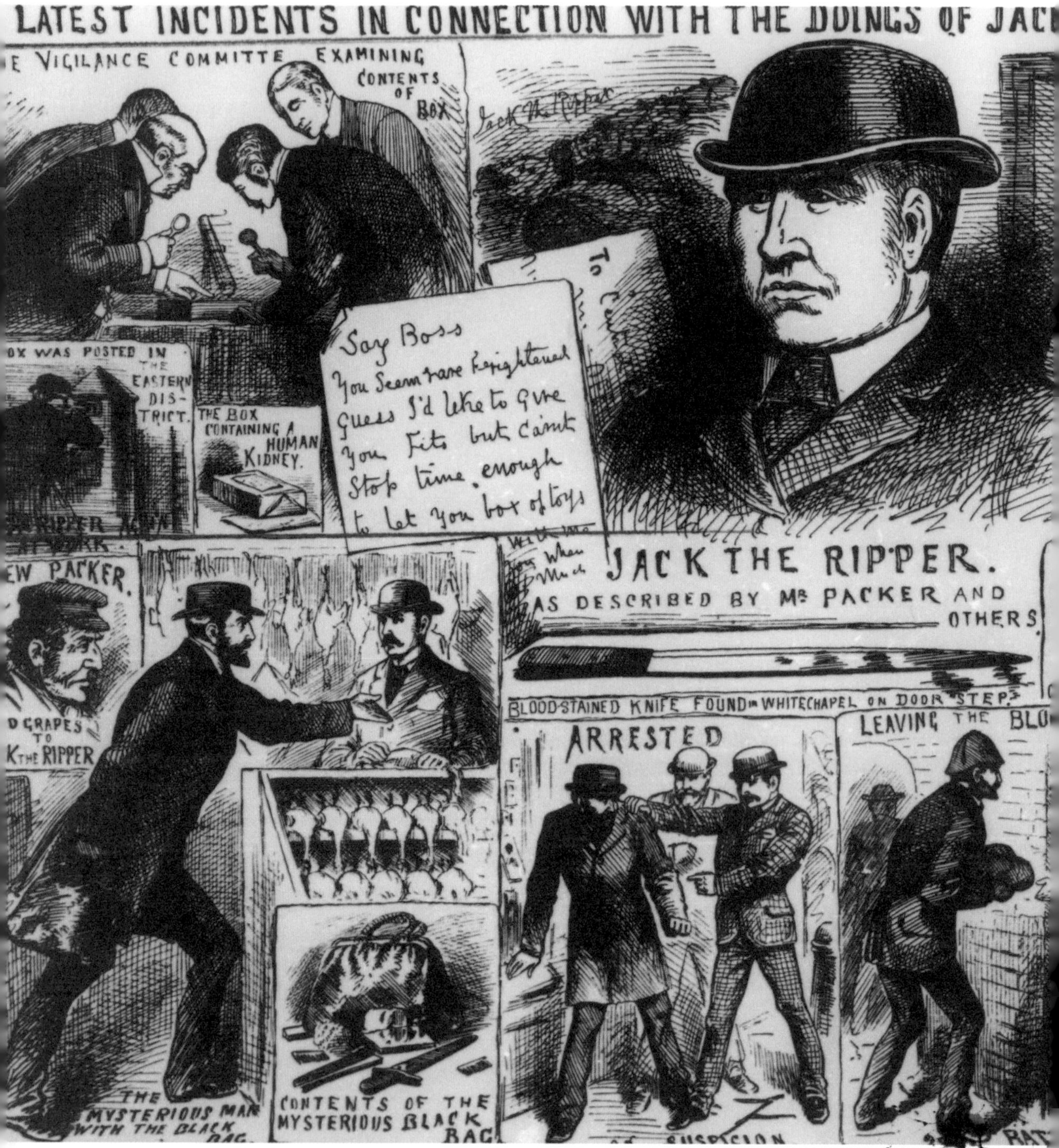

The police were desperate for clues, relying upon witnesses' descriptions, which varied considerably.

KEY WITNESS: ISRAEL SCHWARTZ

At 12.45am on the 30th September, Israel Schwartz walked past the gateway of the International Working-Men's Education Club on Berner Street, where the murder was to take place. He saw a man stop and speak to a woman standing in the gateway, later identified as Elizabeth Stride. Schwartz described the man as 30 years old with a small brown moustache, 5 feet, 5 inches (1.65 m) tall, wearing a dark jacket and trousers and a black peaked cap. He noticed that the broad-shouldered man tried unsuccessfully to pull the woman into the street. The man then turned her around, throwing her to the pavement. Schwartz heard the woman scream three times, but not loudly.

Schwartz did not want to get involved in any argument and, crossing to the other side of the street, noticed for the first time a second man lighting his pipe. The broad-shouldered man who had assaulted Stride called out 'Lipski', which was the name of a Jew who had been convicted of murder and hanged the year before. It was frequently used as a term of abuse to Jews at around this time. Schwartz, a Hungarian immigrant with a strong Jewish appearance, was uncertain whether he or the 'Pipeman' (as he became known) was being addressed as 'Lipski'.

Believing he was being followed by the second man, Israel Schwartz began to run away. Schwartz made a statement to that effect to the Metropolitan Police, recorded by Chief Inspector Swanson. However, this important eyewitness was not called to testify at the inquest of Elizabeth Stride. Using a Hungarian interpreter, he was interviewed by the *Star* newspaper, which published his account of events the next day. Some details differ from the police version, but it may be inferred that Schwartz elaborated on his story so that he did not appear a coward by running away. He had witnessed the assault of a woman who – if it was Elizabeth Stride – would be dead within minutes.

THE MAN WITH
THE BLACK BAG

Apart from Israel Schwartz, who appeared not to have been called to give evidence at the inquest of Elizabeth Stride, there was another significant witness who did not testify – Fanny Mortimer. Mrs. Mortimer lived with her family at 36 Berner Street, just a couple of doors away from the club. She said that on the night of Elizabeth Stride's murder, she had been standing at her front door for 10 or 15 minutes before going inside to get ready for bed in the front room on the ground floor. She heard a pony and cart pass. If this is correct, this is most likely to be Louis Diemschutz, the jewellery trader who was returning home to the club at number 40 Berner Street – at 1.00am.

Fanny Mortimer stated that, while standing outside, "the only person whom I had seen pass through the street previously was a young man carrying a black shiny bag, who walked very fast down the street from Commercial Road." The man carrying the black bag was Leon Goldstein of 22 Christian Street, who presented himself at Leman Street police station the day after the murder. Having spent time at a coffee shop in Spectacle Alley on the south side of Whitechapel High Street, where he collected empty cigarette boxes, he was returning home with the packets in his black bag.

Doubts were raised about inconsistencies in Fanny Mortimer's varied accounts, but the story of the man with the black shiny bag appears consistent. The problem was that Leon Goldstein was not the murderer. However, the connection between the murderer and a black bag had been made – and the black doctor's bag persists in many people's vision of the Ripper even today.

JACK THE RIPPER.
AS DESCRIBED BY Mᵣˢ PACKER AND OTHERS.

NTS OF THE
RIOUS BLACK
BAG

The "black bag" – carrying the murderer's knife – is a popular
part of Ripper mythology.

The inquest of Elizabeth Stride took place in Cable Street.

INQUEST ON FIFTH VICTIM AT ST GEORES IN THE EAST

INSPECTOR REID

THE INQUEST

The inquest for the death of Elizabeth Stride began on 1st October 1888 in Cable Street, at the hall of St George-in-the-East. Adjourned four times, it finally came to a close on 23rd October.

The whole process was drawn out unnecessarily due to some simple errors. Mrs. Mary Malcolm categorically identified Stride's body as her sister, Elizabeth Watts, on the first day of the inquest. The police and the coroner, Wynne Edwin Baxter, were unconvinced by her identification. The real Elizabeth Watts arrived, proving for certain that Mrs. Malcolm was mistaken. Charles Preston, a barber resident at 32 Flower and Dean Street eventually identified the body – correctly this time – as Elizabeth Stride. He had last seen the victim in the lodging house on the evening of 29th September 1888.

The eyewitness account of Israel Schwartz, particularly based on his police testimony on the 30th September given at Leman Street police station, appears to be of great importance to the subsequent murder of Elizabeth Stride. However, there is no definitive record of Schwartz testifying at the inquest. This is one of the many great mysteries and possible oversights concerning the Whitechapel murders.

It is curious to note, therefore, that a memo from Assistant Commissioner of the Metropolitan Police Dr. Robert Anderson alludes to Schwartz testifying, when the police are querying the meaning of 'Lipski' (shouted out by Stride's assailant). Anderson may be incorrect in his assertion, but it is also possible that the press decided not to report this information, believing that it might inflame further anti-Semitic feeling in the Whitechapel area.

Once more, the jury returned a verdict of 'wilful murder', but the police were no closer to catching the murderer. The inquest commented that there had been no 'skilful mutilation' as in the cases of Nichols and Chapman. Perhaps the murderer had been disturbed on this busy night, before he had the chance to spend time finishing off the victim as he seemed to enjoy.

This police sketch shows where the body of the fourth victim was found in Mitre Square.

CRIME SCENE #4: MITRE SQUARE

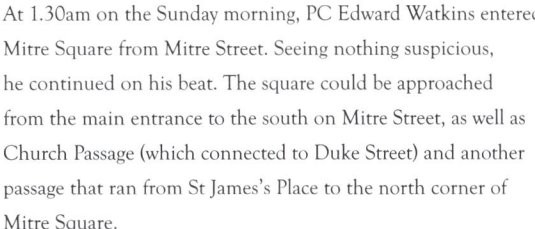

Sunday 30th September 1888 was to be an eventful morning in the Whitechapel murder inquiry. Police had already discovered the body of Elizabeth Stride at Dutfield's Yard. Only 45 minutes later, a second corpse was found.

At 1.30am on the Sunday morning, PC Edward Watkins entered Mitre Square from Mitre Street. Seeing nothing suspicious, he continued on his beat. The square could be approached from the main entrance to the south on Mitre Street, as well as Church Passage (which connected to Duke Street) and another passage that ran from St James's Place to the north corner of Mitre Square.

PC Watkins returned to the square 15 minutes later, approaching again from the Mitre Street entrance. He flashed his light into the dark southwest corner, a popular haunt for prostitutes and their clients. There he lit up the mutilated body of a prostitute, Catherine Eddowes, lying on her back in a pool of blood. The policeman later told the *Star* newspaper, "She was ripped up like a pig in the market... I have been in the force a long while, but I never saw such a sight." There was, of course, no sign of her client, the murderer.

Watkins ran to Kearley and Tonge's warehouse on the other side of the square to find nightwatchman George James Morris, a former Metropolitan police officer, saying, "For God's sake mate, come to assist me... another woman cut up to pieces." While PC Watkins remained with the corpse, George Morris found PC James Harvey and PC Frederick Holland, and told them of the horrific discovery in Mitre Square. PC Holland went to Jewry Street, Aldgate, to fetch Dr. George William Sequeira, who on examination of the body, believed that the woman had not been dead for more than 15 minutes.

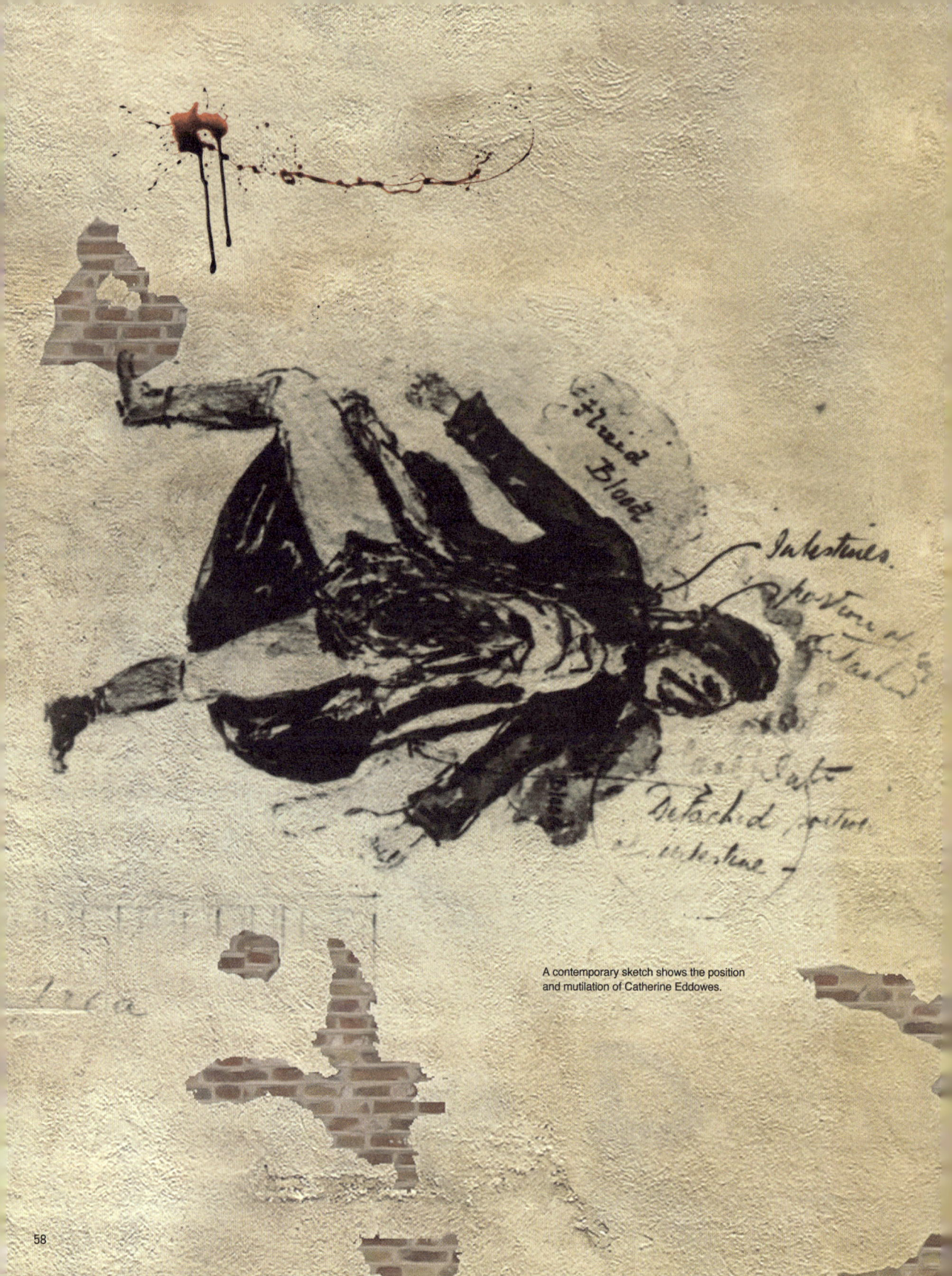

A contemporary sketch shows the position and mutilation of Catherine Eddowes.

POST-MORTEM OF THE FOURTH VICTIM

Dr. George William Sequeira waited for the City Police Surgeon, Dr. Frederick Gordon Brown, to examine the body just after 2.00am. It was a bloodthirsty attack. The throat of the victim had been cut, and there was a handkerchief tied around the neck. Her abdomen was exposed and the intestines had been scooped out and draped over the right shoulder. A section of intestines about 24 inches (60 cm) in length had been cut from the body and placed between the left flank and arm. The murderer had horribly mutilated the woman's face. There was no blood on the front of the victim's clothes and no spurting of blood on the ground, although a quantity of blood had collected on the left side of the neck, where the throat had been cut. After examination *in situ*, the body was removed and taken to the City Mortuary in Golden Lane.

Dr. Brown continued his examination of Catherine Eddowes' body at the mortuary.

For the first time, the Whitechapel killer had mutilated the face of his victim. He cut through the lower left eyelid, repeating a cut to the right eyelid. A deep cut into the cheekbone began at the bridge of the nose down to the angle of the jaw on the right side of the cheek. The tip of the nose had been sliced off and there were further incisions to either cheek. A deep gash to the throat was 6–7 inches (15–18 cm) in length: Dr. Brown found that death was caused by haemorrhage, due to the severing of the left carotid artery.

Further mutilations, most likely carried out after death included: laying open the abdomen; stabbing the liver; and a variety of incisions and stabs to the abdomen and genitals. The womb was cut through and removed. Perhaps the most significant feature was the removal of the left kidney – Dr. Brown believed that only someone with anatomical knowledge could have done this.

A CLUE TO THE RIPPER'S IDENTITY

Detective Daniel Halse of the City Police accompanied the body of Catherine Eddowes, the fourth victim, to the mortuary. As the mortuary keeper stripped her body, Halse noticed that a portion of her apron was missing. Detective Halse returned to Mitre Square, where he learned that a piece of apron had been found, not far from the crime scene, at Goulston Street. At just before 3.00am on his beat, PC Alfred Long had discovered the missing portion from Eddowes' apron. A corner of it was smeared with blood. The material was lying on the floor of a stairway leading to 108–119 Wentworth Dwellings on Goulston Street.

Above the piece of apron, on the black brick surface of the building wall, was a message written in white chalk. Accounts differ to the exact wording. PC Long noted down the words in his notebook as, "The Jews are the men that will not be blamed for nothing". PC Halse, however, recorded them as, "The Juwes are not the men that will be blamed for nothing". Due to differences in wording, the meaning was not clear. Although the message was found directly above the bloody apron, it was uncertain whether the chalk message, now known as the Goulston Street graffito, was associated in any way with the crimes. Should the Jews (or Juwes) be cleared or blamed for the recent murder (or murders). Was the murderer leaving a calling card?

Ambiguous or not, the chalk message was soon removed by the police, at the instruction of Sir Charles Warren, the Metropolitan Police Commissioner. Warren and other accompanying officers were concerned that people at nearby Petticoat Lane market (on Middlesex Street) would see the message and that this could revive anti-Semitic feeling provoked by investigations surrounding an early Jewish suspect known as 'Leather Apron'. City Police requests to photograph the message as evidence were unaccountably ignored by the Metropolitan Police officers.

The Jews are the men that will not be blamed for nothing

A piece of bloodied apron seemed to point to a
message which may have been a clue to the Ripper.

THE LIFE OF CATHERINE EDDOWES

Catherine Eddowes was born in Wolverhampton in 1842, the daughter of a tinplate varnisher, George Eddowes. From the age of about 20, Catherine lived in Birmingham with Thomas Conway, who was receiving an army pension from the 18th Royal Irish Regiment. They were not registered as married but had three children together: Annie, George and a second son. Catherine was remembered as an intelligent individual who became more hot-headed when she drank heavily, which seemed to be a regular occurrence. The couple split up in 1880, with Catherine taking her daughter Annie with her. Annie soon married, moving around south London several times. Annoyed by her mother's scrounging ways, Annie deliberately avoided her.

Catherine took up with an Irish porter named John Kelly, and became known as 'Kate Kelly', lodging at Cooney's, number 55 Flower and Dean Street, and staying with him until her demise. John Kelly and others from Cooney's described her as cheerful and good natured.

No-one claimed to know that she was a prostitute. At the time of her death, Catherine was 46 years old and 4 feet, 11 inches (1.50 m) tall, with dark auburn hair and hazel eyes. She had TC – for Thomas Conway – tattooed on her left forearm.

In September 1888, Catherine travelled to Kent with Kelly to pick hops, but after poor weather that year, most of the crops had been wiped out. The couple returned to London on the 27th September, staying at the casual ward in Shoe Lane. Here, Catherine allegedly told the superintendent, "I have come back to earn the reward offered for the apprehension of the Whitechapel Murderer. I think I know him." The man advised her to watch out that she was not murdered, to which she replied, "Oh, no fear of that." There is no way of knowing whether or not she knew the man – or could capture him – but unfortunately for her, at just after 1.30am on 30th September 1888, Catherine Eddowes was in the wrong place at the wrong time.

Catherine Eddowes was unlucky to have been in London
on the night of her murder – she had returned early.

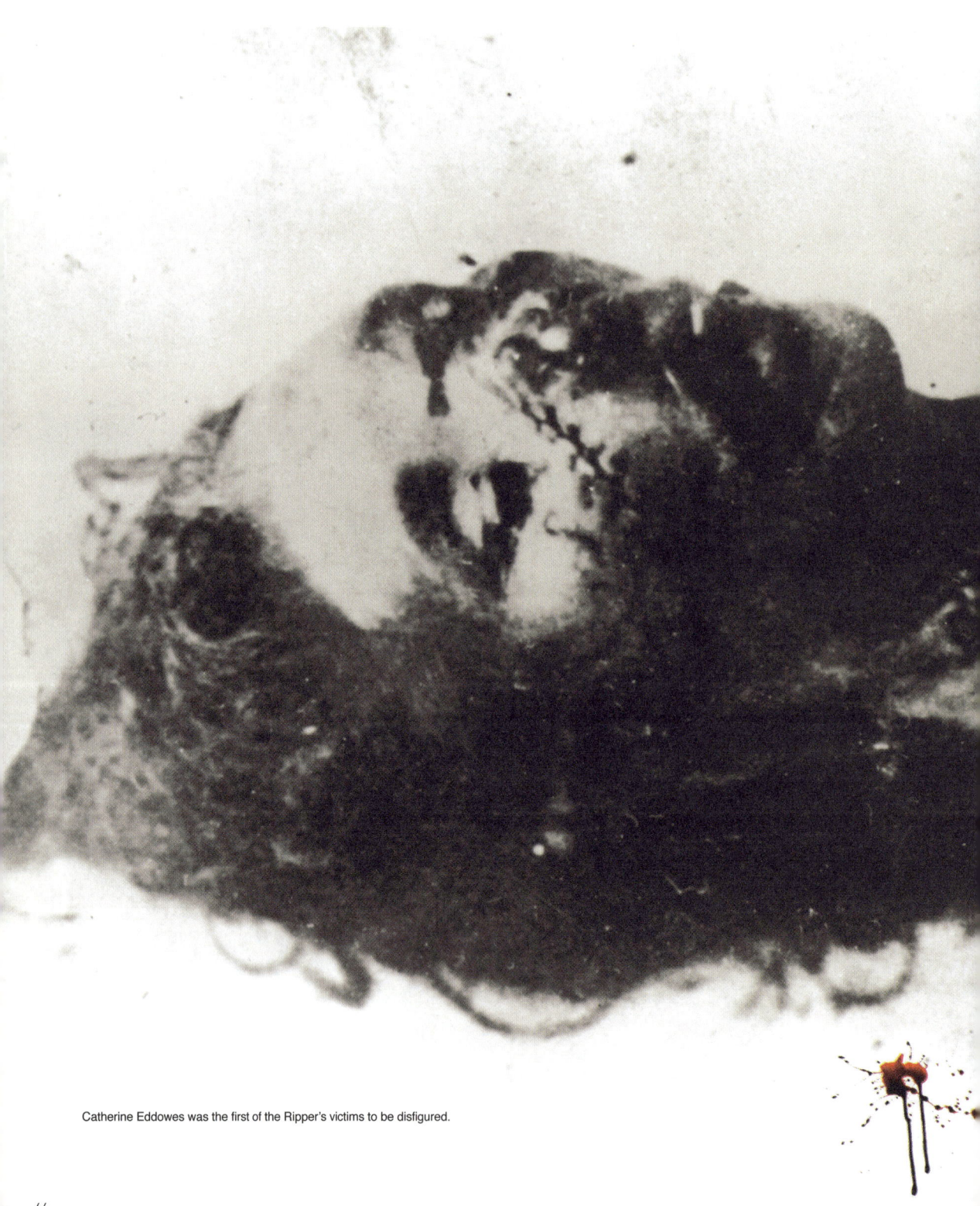

Catherine Eddowes was the first of the Ripper's victims to be disfigured.

THE LAST HOURS OF CATHERINE EDDOWES

Catherine Eddowes left John Kelly in Houndsditch in the early afternoon of Saturday 29th September 1888, planning to find her daughter in Bermondsey to get some money from her. She promised Kelly that she would be back before 4.00pm. It was not surprising that Catherine did not find her daughter, because she had been living in Southwark for at least a year.

Catherine Eddowes was next seen in Aldgate High Street, causing a disturbance by impersonating a fire engine. Somehow, she had managed to get hold of some money – and spent it on drink. She was arrested by PC Louis Robinson and PC George Simmons for being drunk and disorderly, and taken to Bishopsgate police station. Asked her name, Eddowes replied, "Nothing", and was put in a cell at about 8.30pm by the station sergeant, James Byfield, until she became sober. Twenty minutes later, PC Robinson looked in on her, noticing that she was sound asleep, reeking of alcohol.

An hour later, PC George Hutt came on duty at Bishopsgate police station. He regularly inspected the cells and also engaged in conversation with Catherine. By 12.15am on Sunday the 30th September, Hutt noticed that she was awake in her cell, singing to herself. At 12.30am, Catherine asked when she would be able to leave. His reply was, "When you are capable of taking care of yourself."

By 12.55am, Catherine appeared to have sobered up and was allowed out of her cell. Having found out what the time was, she told Hutt that she would get "a damn fine hiding" as soon as she got home. He replied, "And serve you right. You have no right to get drunk." PC Hutt asked her name, to which she replied, "Mary Ann Kelly", giving a false address too. Hutt asked Catherine to close the outer door of the police station as she left. Her last words were, "All right. Goodnight, old cock."

KEY WITNESS: JOSEPH LAWENDE

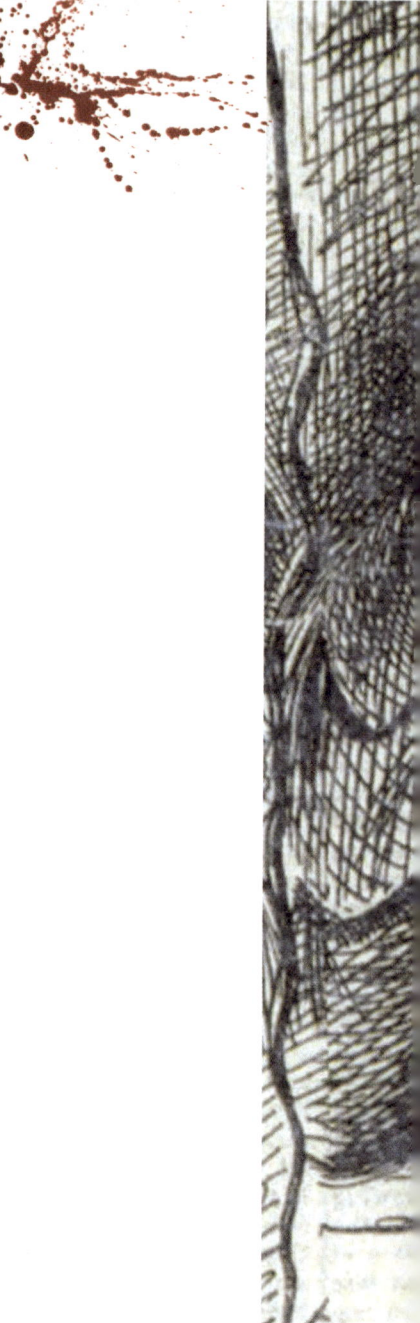

At 1.35am on Sunday 30th September 1888, Joseph Lawende was leaving the Imperial Club at 16–17 Duke Street with Harry Harris and Joseph Hyam Levy. They saw a couple talking at the entrance to Church Passage, leading to Mitre Square and Levy said, "I don't like going home by myself when I see these sorts of characters about. I'm off!" Both Levy and Harris maintained that they could not recognise the man or woman, although Levy later identified Eddowes' clothes as those worn by the woman in the passageway. Although Levy and Harris were not very observant, Lawende is a key eyewitness: he identified Eddowes from her clothing (black bonnet and jacket) at the police station, but he also took note of the man's appearance. Within minutes of being seen, Catherine Eddowes was lying dead in Mitre Square, and her body discovered by the police at 1.45am, so his testimony is of vital importance.

Joseph Lawende walked a little apart from the other two witnesses, so he happened to observe slightly more in the passageway than his friends from the Club. He stated that the woman faced the man, but that "I saw only her back." He did not overhear their conversation, but "they did not appear to be in an angry mood." Lawende observed that the woman had her hand on the man's chest, not in a frightened manner of pushing him away, but she was touching him in a friendly way.

Lawende described the man as about 30 years old, 5 feet, 8 inches (1.73 m) tall, with a shabby, sailor-like appearance. He was wearing a loose, pepper-and-salt coloured jacket and grey cloth cap with a peak, as well as a reddish neckerchief. He had a fair complexion and a moustache. Despite his description, Lawende was not sure that he would recognise the man if he saw him again.

Joseph Lawende provided a thorough description of the man he saw at the entrance to Church Passage, but was it the murderer?

THE INQUEST FOR CATHERINE EDDOWES

The inquest began on 4th October 1888 at Golden Lane
Mortuary, presided over by Samuel Frederick Langham, the City
coroner. Lasting two days, the inquest was adjourned until the
11th October to close the case. On the second day, the jury gave
their verdict as "wilful murder by some person unknown".

As the Elizabeth Stride inquest had started earlier than that
of Catherine Eddowes, comparisons could be made between
the two murders. Those present at the Eddowes' inquest
debated whether the horrific cuts and mutilations to her body
and face demonstrated that the perpetrator had anatomical
knowledge. Both Dr. Sequeira and Dr. Saunders thought that
the mutilations did not show that the killer had great anatomical
skill, whereas Dr. Brown – on the evidence of the killer's ability
to remove a kidney – believed that the murderer *did* possess
a certain amount of knowledge. In conclusion, Dr. Brown
surmised that although he may not be a surgeon or doctor, the
killer could have been a slaughterer of animals. From the timing
of the second murder on the 30th September, the method of
killing was brutally efficient and the murderer carried out the
further mutilation with great speed, managing to extract both
the womb and one kidney.

THE WHITECHAPEL MYSTERY.

Catherine Eddowes pictured before and after her death.

The two murders in the early morning of Sunday the 30th September were thought to be connected: a double murder mystery. Although the murderer of Elizabeth Stride in Dutfield's Yard had not attempted to disembowel his victim, it was possible that he had been disturbed (perhaps by Louis Diemschutz) after slitting her throat. He had travelled from the first murder site to the second, in Mitre Square, without arousing the attention of policemen carrying out their regular beats. Furthermore, after dispatching Catherine Eddowes, the murderer was able to escape from Mitre Square carrying a knife, a kidney, a womb and a piece of apron.

The 1959 film *Jack the Ripper* recreates the panic in London streets at the peak of the Ripper scare.

THE KILLER HAS A NAME

The double murder on Sunday 30th September 1888 set in motion a series of events that began to obscure police investigations to catch the Whitechapel Murderer. Fearful of an invisible killer, the public became incensed that the police and government were not doing enough to capture him. Public opinion, fuelled by the press, criticised the Home Secretary Henry Matthews and Metropolitan Police Commissioner Sir Charles Warren in particular for not offering a reward for information to help catch the killer. Although neither was against the idea, the popular policy of offering rewards had been abandoned four years earlier. Their political mistake was in not explaining why no reward was being offered for information leading to the arrest and conviction of the murderer. The *Star* said that "if the murders had happened in Mayfair we should have had rewards fast enough."

Offers of help were not unforthcoming. Within hours of the discovery of Catherine Eddowes' corpse (the first murder on the City of London's patch), Sir James Fraser, the Commissioner of the City of London Police offered a £500 reward. Soon afterwards the Lord Mayor of London offered a reward of the same amount on behalf of the Corporation of London. Wealthy businessman Samuel Montagu had also offered a reward: in total, a reward figure of £1,200 was available.

Following offers of rewards, there was another key development that hampered rather than helped the investigation. Three weeks after second victim Annie Chapman died and the day before the double murder, the Metropolitan Police received a letter (addressed 'Dear Boss'), purporting to be from the Whitechapel Murderer. Hoax or not, it taunted the Metropolitan Police with, "The next job I do I shall clip the lady's ears off and send to the police officers." The letter was signed. Prior to this, the killer did not have a name. Some referred to him as "the Knife". Soon, everyone knew him as *Jack the Ripper.*

CRIME SCENE #5: 13 MILLER'S COURT

While other prostitutes had their throats slit in the open air, the fifth victim of Jack the Ripper had different surroundings. Mary Jane Kelly was killed indoors, in her own bed. Her address at number 13 Miller's Court was situated off one of the East End's most notorious streets. Sometimes known as 'Dosser's Street', it was of course Dorset Street. Canon Samuel A. Barnett of St Jude's Vicarage described 'the hells of Dorset Street', which he saw as the 'centre of evil'. He could not have foreseen the horror that in the early hours of Friday 9th November 1888 proved his description to be so accurate.

At about 10.45am on that Friday morning, Thomas Bowyer headed up the grubby passageway leading from Dorset Street to Miller's Court. His boss, John McCarthy of 27 Dorset Street had sent Bowyer to 13 Miller's Court to collect Mary Jane Kelly's rent: she owed McCarthy 30 shillings. Bowyer knocked twice on the door, and receiving no reply, went around the corner to the windows of the same room, where he noticed a pane of glass was missing. He put his hand carefully through the empty frame and pulled aside a curtain to look inside. In the dark room he saw lumps of flesh on the bedside table. On the bed he saw a body, butchered beyond recognition. Bowyer ran to McCarthy's shop at the end of the passageway. McCarthy went with Bowyer to see for himself, although he would have wished never to have looked at the horrifying vision through the window:

"The sight we saw, I cannot drive away from my mind. It looked more like the work of a devil than of a man. I had heard a great deal about the Whitechapel murders, but I declare to God I had never expected to see such a sight as this. The whole scene is more than I can describe. I hope I may never see such a sight again."

Dorset Street: the entrance to Miller's Court
was by the third lamp on the left.

THE ILLUSTRATED

LAW COURTS AND WEEKLY RECORD

SATURDAY, OCTOBER 20, 1888.

IDENTS RELATING TO THE EAST END MURDERS

TRIAL OF BLOODHOUNDS

SIR C.

There was a long delay waiting – but the bloodhounds never arrived at the crime scene.

WAITING FOR THE BLOODHOUNDS

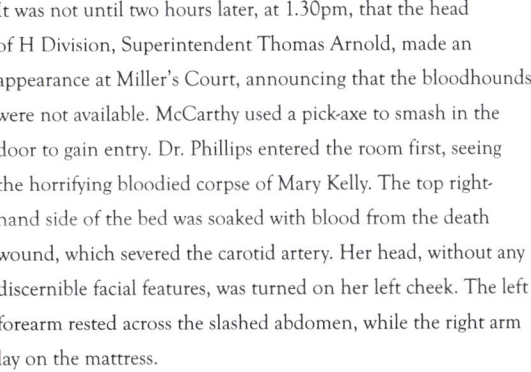

Summoned by John McCarthy and Thomas Bowyer, Inspector Walter Beck arrived at the crime scene from nearby Commercial Street police station. Like the two earlier witnesses, Beck peered through the broken window into number 13. Several constables came to his aid, sealing off the nearby streets, while he sent for police surgeon Dr. George Bagster Phillips who viewed the body through the window, at 11.15am. Fifteen minutes later, Inspector Frederick George Abberline arrived and Dr. Phillips suggested that they did not enter the room until bloodhounds were brought to the scene of the crime. Residents were questioned and a photographer took pictures – again, through the window.

It was not until two hours later, at 1.30pm, that the head of H Division, Superintendent Thomas Arnold, made an appearance at Miller's Court, announcing that the bloodhounds were not available. McCarthy used a pick-axe to smash in the door to gain entry. Dr. Phillips entered the room first, seeing the horrifying bloodied corpse of Mary Kelly. The top right-hand side of the bed was soaked with blood from the death wound, which severed the carotid artery. Her head, without any discernible facial features, was turned on her left cheek. The left forearm rested across the slashed abdomen, while the right arm lay on the mattress.

Half an hour later, Dr. Phillips and Dr. Bond examined the body more carefully. The throat had been sliced deeply from ear to ear. The breasts were cut off. The heart was missing. The legs were placed wide apart and the top layers of the thighs and abdomen removed and placed on the table. The uterus, kidney and one breast were placed under the head, while the other breast was near the right foot. Liver, intestines and spleen were placed around the body on the bed. Dr. Bond estimated the time of death at between 1.00am and 2.00am, as *rigor mortis* had set in.

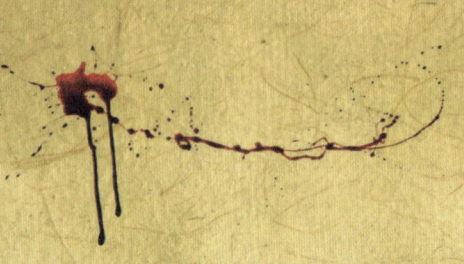

THE LIFE OF MARY JANE KELLY

Much of Mary Jane Kelly's early life remains sketchy, and what is known cannot be confirmed as conclusive. She was born in Limerick, in 1863 and, as a young child, moved with her father John Kelly to Wales, when he took a job as a foreman at an ironworks. In 1879 she married a collier John Davies, who died in a pit explosion two or three years later. Mary soon moved to stay with a cousin in Cardiff, where she became a prostitute. By 1884, she was in London working in a high-class brothel in the West End. One of her gentlemen clients took her to Paris, but she shortly returned to London, sometimes using the more exotic French-sounding name Marie Jeanette Kelly.

Mary met a porter, Joseph Barnett, at Billingsgate Market on Good Friday, 8th April 1887. The following day they decided to live together, lodging at a variety of addresses within the so-called 'wicked quarter mile' of Whitechapel, around Flower and Dean Street. The couple shared a cramped single room at her final address at 13 Miller's Court for a rent of four shillings and sixpence a week. Joseph Barnett lost his job, and with their rent several weeks in arrears, Mary returned to prostitution. She also let other prostitutes use their room, which caused Joseph to leave shortly before Mary's death.

Life was tough for Mary Jane Kelly. Owing rent, she had to fall back on prostitution.

At the time of her death, Mary was only 25 years old, and much younger than the other women murdered by Jack the Ripper. Also known as 'Fair Emma' due to her complexion and hair, she was 5 foot, 7 inches (1.70 m) tall, with long blonde hair. Other nicknames included 'Black Mary' (some reports mention her quick temper) and 'Ginger'.

THE LAST HOURS OF MARY JANE KELLY

On Thursday 8th November 1888, Joseph Barnett visited Mary Kelly around 7.30pm. Although the couple had separated, Barnett still called in on her most days. He left Kelly at approximately 8.00pm. Mystery surrounds the final hours of Mary Jane Kelly. Although there are several sightings, no-one knows for certain what happened, because some of the sightings are contradictory, with none confirmed.

At 11.45pm Mary Ann Cox, a prostitute who also lived in Miller's Court, saw Kelly as she turned into Dorset Street from Commercial Street. Kelly was with a man about 35 years old with a thick carrotty moustache and shabby overcoat. She followed them into Miller's Court. Cox and Kelly said "Goodnight" to one another, and the couple disappeared into number 13. Cox heard Kelly singing the same song, over and over again. Another neighbour, Catherine Pickett, was annoyed by Kelly's singing at around 12.30am.

From 1.00am, another prostitute Elizabeth Prater was standing at the Miller's Court entrance for about 30 minutes. She saw no-one enter or leave Miller's Court. Another witness, who appears to be more reliable was George Hutchinson. He chatted to Mary Kelly in the street at 2.00am, then saw her disappear with a stranger – with a different appearance to the man with the 'carrotty' moustache – into Miller's Court.

Cries of "Murder!" recounted by Sarah Lewis at around 4.00am were ignored, with such cries not uncommon in the area. At 8.00am a tailor named Maurice Lewis saw Kelly leave her room, returning minutes later. At about the same time, neighbour Caroline Maxwell chatted to Kelly outside McCarthy's shop. Kelly complained of the "horrors of drink", and Maxwell suggested she should go to the Britannia for the hair of the dog. At 8.30am, Maxwell saw Kelly talking to a stranger outside the pub. At 10.00am, Maurice Lewis believed he saw Kelly drinking inside the Britannia. The later times of these sightings are difficult to reconcile with the likely time of the murder.

IT WI
OF THI
OF THE MURD

ROUGH THE BROKEN PANES
DOW THAT THE BODY
OMAN WAS FIRST SEEN

Mary Jane Kelly allowed Jack the Ripper into her lodgings at
13 Miller's Court.

THE INQUEST

The rent collector was the first to see the body of Mary Jane Kelly.

Mary Jane Kelly's inquest took place on 12th November 1888 at Shoreditch Town Hall, with Dr. Roderick Macdonald, coroner for the North-East Middlesex district in charge of proceedings. Although coroner Wynne Edwin Baxter made an attempt to claim the Kelly inquest, he was unsuccessful because Kelly's corpse had been removed from Miller's Court to Shoreditch Mortuary – placing it under Dr. Macdonald's jurisdiction.

Dr. Roderick Macdonald was criticised for the speed and methods of dealing with the inquest. Beginning at 11.00am, it appeared that this would be another long inquest – in line with the earlier Ripper inquests. The coroner listened to the brisk testimonies of local residents, but dismissed those that did not fit in with Dr. Bond's estimation of death at between 1.00am and 2.00am (A later independent medical report was to estimate the time of Kelly's death to be around 3.30am to 4.00am). Macdonald intimated that neither Maurice Lewis nor Caroline Maxwell could have seen Kelly at 8.00am or later.

The coroner stated that he would not cover all the medical details at this stage. The *Daily Telegraph* reported that, after the evidence given by Dr. Phillips, "the jury had no questions to ask at this stage, and it was understood that more detailed evidence of a future examination would be given at a future hearing." However, to everyone's surprise, the coroner cut short any further details or examination, and turning to the jury asked if they had heard enough to reach their verdict. Apparently persuaded by the coroner's direction, the jury reached the familiar verdict of "wilful murder by person or persons unknown". The coroner had wrapped up the inquest within a short single day.

The management of the inquest by Macdonald was generally criticised, and the *Daily Telegraph* urged the Home Secretary to order a fresh inquiry. It was thought that such mishandling of a huge murder investigation might even lead to a possible acquittal of the murderer, if he was ever caught.

KEY WITNESS:
GEORGE HUTCHINSON

Due to the brevity of the flawed inquest by Dr. Roderick Macdonald, one vital witness did not emerge until after the jury's verdict. George Hutchinson made a statement to the police (at about 6.00pm on the 12th November) in which he said he had met the victim at 2.00am on the 9th November, making him quite possibly the last person to see her alive. Except her killer.

George Hutchinson had known Mary Kelly for about three years: he was on friendly terms with her, occasionally giving her a few shillings. On the morning of her death, Hutchinson was walking up Commercial Street, in the direction of Dorset Street, when he met Mary Kelly near Thrawl Street. She asked to borrow money, but Hutchinson replied that he had spent it all going to Romford. She said, "Good morning. I must go and find some money." Kelly walked to Thrawl Street, passing a man who stood on the corner. Hutchinson noticed the man place his hand on Kelly's shoulder and spoke to her. They both laughed, Kelly said "All right", and the man replied, "You will be all right for what I have told you."

About 5 feet, 7 inches (1.70 m) tall, the man was around 35, well dressed and with a Jewish appearance. He had dark hair with a slight moustache curled up at the ends. He wore a long dark coat and a dark felt hat. Hutchinson was able to give an incredibly detailed description to the police, right down to the man's button boots and gaiters with white buttons. He noticed that he carried a parcel with a strap around it. Hutchinson was curious to see his face and bent down to take a better look at him, as they passed outside the Queen's Head public house.
He followed the couple down Dorset Street and watched them as they stood outside Miller's Court entrance. Kelly said, "All right, my dear. Come along, you will be comfortable" and they kissed, before disappearing up the passageway. Hutchinson waited for 45 minutes – no-one emerged.

"HE TURNED AND LOOKED AT ME."

Eyewitness George Hutchinson was suspicious of the stranger with Mary Jane Kelly.

Some descriptions of Jack the Ripper were of a short, stout man.

OTHER MURDERS

Ripperologists and others with more than a passing interest in criminology, will continue to debate how many of the murders in Whitechapel towards the turn of the 19th century were committed by Jack the Ripper. Most follow Sir Melville Macnaghten's pronouncement of "5 victims – & 5 victims only" as helpful, if not as absolute as he intended. Some argue that the third victim Elizabeth Stride was not mutilated. Others believe that the fifth victim, Mary Jane Kelly, showed a different *modus operandi*, with the killer butchering the prostitute in her own bed. There may have been fewer victims, there may well have been more. We shall probably never know for sure. Let us return to a murder that happened in early April 1888, the year of the frightening 'Autumn of Terror'.

Emma Elizabeth Smith was attacked at about 1.30am on 3rd April 1888 by three men outside Taylor Brothers' Mustard and Cocoa factory in Brick Lane. She later died at Whitechapel Hospital. According to H Division's Chief Inspector Walter Dew, who believed she was an early victim of Jack the Ripper, Emma Smith was something of a mystery. She hid her past, even from her close friends: she would tell them that she had been a widow for several years and had severed connections with her former life. One time she confided to a friend, "They would not understand now any more than they understood then. I must live somehow."

Emma Smith was about 45 years old, 5 feet, 2 inches (1.57 m) tall, with light brown hair. She was an alcoholic and could be bad-tempered when drunk. Very little is known about the attack, partly because Emma Smith herself was so reticent. Many believed the assault was carried out by a violent gang from The Nichol, a slum at the north end of Brick Lane, who extorted money from prostitutes. The jury's verdict was "wilful murder by some person or persons unknown".

MARTHA TABRAM

The murder of Martha Tabram on 7th August 1888 was
barbaric, taking place in George Yard off Wentworth Street.
Its East End location, just around the corner from the assault
on Emma Smith in Brick Lane, linked the murders in many
people's minds. However, unlike the earlier assault, the brutal
murder of Martha Tabram appeared to have no motive.

Martha Tabram was out for the evening of 6th August 1888,
with fellow prostitute 'Pearly Poll', as Mary Ann Connolly was
commonly known. Connolly said that they were picked up by
two guardsmen and the foursome went on a pub crawl together
from around 10.00pm. One witness, Ann Morris, Tabram's
sister-in-law, claimed to have seen Martha Tabram enter a pub on
Whitechapel High Street, probably the White Swan. It is likely
that Ann Morris was a reliable witness, but her statement makes
no mention of the two soldiers.

Mary Ann Connolly and Martha Tabram left the pub at
around 11.45pm and headed east up Whitechapel High Street
past Commercial Street with the soldiers. While Connolly
disappeared with her corporal up Angel Alley (parallel to
Osborn Street and Brick Lane), Martha Tabram went with the
private into an adjacent narrow passageway, situated next to the
White Hart public house. The alleyway led into George Yard
(today's Gunthorpe Street). At the top of the street, almost at the
junction with Wentworth Street, Martha Tabram was stabbed
to death 39 times in the stairwell of George Yard buildings.
A tenant of the block, John Saunders Reeves, discovered her
bloodied body at a 4.45am. The post-mortem found that Martha
Tabram had been stabbed in the lungs, heart, liver, stomach,
spleen, breasts and genitals. It was concluded that the wounds
could have been made by the short blade of a bayonet. No-one
was ever convicted of the murders of either Emma Smith or
Martha Tabram.

Stabbed many times, Martha Tabram was murdered in George Yard.

The murder of "Claypipe Annie" led some to believe
that she was another Jack the Ripper victim.

FURTHER SCARES

The 'Canonical Five' victims – Nichols, Chapman, Stride, Eddowes and Kelly – display similarities. The murders also show escalation of brutality and an audacious swagger. From the ritual throat slitting and mutilation of early victims, then the double murder, to the ferocious finale of Mary Jane Kelly, the Ripper gains momentum in each attack. Then it goes quiet.

As 'Saucy Jacky' as he was sometimes known (see page 111) was never caught, no-one knows why the murders suddenly stop. At the time of the Autumn of Terror, the murder of Mary Jane Kelly was described by some newspapers as the seventh Whitechapel murder. And the killer was still on the loose.

There were scares that Jack the Ripper was back. Eight months after the horrors of 13 Miller's Court, another woman was murdered in Whitechapel. At 12.50am on 17th July 1889, PC Walter Andrews discovered a body in Castle Alley. Her throat had been cut, her skirts raised and abdomen mutilated: it all bore the hallmark of the Ripper. An old clay pipe was found under her body and she was soon identified as 40-year-old Alice 'Claypipe Annie' McKenzie. Her left carotid artery had been severed, similar to the earlier Ripper victims, but the wounds were not deep, or right through to the spinal column, leading Dr. Phillips to see this as just another murder. However, Dr. Bond believed this was another Ripper victim.

Less than two months later, on 10th September 1889, another body was found. This time, a naked female trunk was discovered under railway arches in Pinchin Street. She was never formally identified. However, this killing was unlike any *bona fide* Jack the Ripper murder. After a respite in 1890, there was one more scare to come. At 2.15am on 13th February 1891, PC Ernest Thompson discovered the body of Frances Coles, a 26-year-old prostitute, in Swallow Gardens – again under railway arches. Her throat had recently been slit and she died soon after. She had no abdominal wounds and Dr. Phillips thought that this was not the work of Jack the Ripper.

THE INVESTIGATORS

WHY WAS HE
NEVER CAUGHT?

Jack the Ripper was an extraordinary killer: today, he is part myth, part monster. But once the fictional layers are peeled away, there is an ordinary person. He was a vicious murderer who had ample opportunity to kill. He could come and go, murdering his victims, and disappear as if by magic, blending in with the crowd. And that's the problem with Jack the Ripper – he probably appeared very ordinary.

Everyone knows that Jack the Ripper evaded capture. Over the years, the Victorian police have received plenty of criticism for failing to catch him, but they were also censured by their contemporaries for not doing enough. They were nowhere near capturing him, but at the same time they faced a monumental task – and perhaps 'Saucy Jacky' was lucky.

Today, criminal investigations are able to use sophisticated tools of crime detection, such as DNA profiling and advanced forensics, making it much easier to prove that a person has been at the scene of a crime. However, in 1888, even fingerprinting was still unknown by police forces in the UK, and not introduced to New Scotland Yard until the turn of the century (resulting in the first conviction using fingerprint evidence in 1902).

Police officers were overwhelmed. Following each new murder, panic would take hold of the Whitechapel neighbourhood. Jack the Ripper would carve up his victim and make his exit, apparently leaving no trace. Jack the Ripper was helped by the maze of alleyways and dark passages – not only when he murdered his victims, but also as he made his escape. The Victorian police may well have struggled to cope, but not one person in over 100 years has been any closer to solving the mystery of who Jack the Ripper was.

Jack the Ripper was difficult to catch: no known motive and no real clues.

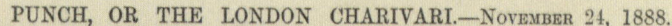

EXTREMES MEET.

Sir Edmund. "MY DEAR WARREN, YOU DID TOO MUCH!"   Sir Charles. "AND YOU, MY DEAR HENDERSO

Mr. Punch (*sotto voce*). "H'M!—SORRY FOR THE *NEW MAN*-!!"

Punch criticises both Henderson and Warren for their handling of
Trafalgar Square riots and the Whitechapel murders.

SIR CHARLES WARREN (1840-1927)

Sir Charles Warren (1840–1927) took over as Metropolitan Police Commissioner in 1886, after the resignation of Sir Edmund Henderson (due to his controversial handling of the Trafalgar Square riots of February 1886). Initially a popular choice, Warren, too, mishandled rioting crowds demonstrating against unemployment in Trafalgar Square in November 1887, known as Bloody Sunday.

Sir Charles Warren had an uneasy relationship with the press, especially due to the growing problem of the Whitechapel murders during the autumn of 1888. Under Warren, the Metropolitan Police were suspicious of press exposure and so appeared guarded. Understandably, the Criminal Investigation Department (CID) wanted to maintain secrecy about the investigation, while newspaper journalists, desperate for a lead, would trail detectives to interview the same people straight after the police.

Warren received particular criticism following the Goulston Street graffito. City of London police were involved because the murder of Catherine Eddowes had taken place in Mitre Square. Meanwhile, an important piece of evidence – part of Eddowes' bloodied apron had been found in Goulston Street (under the jurisdiction of the Metropolitan Police). Both forces were debating what to do with the chalk message, which they worried might stir up anti-Semitic unrest in the area. Sir Charles Warren arrived at the scene around 5.00am and ordered the message to be erased. He overruled PC Halse of the City of London Police, who suggested taking a photograph as soon as the light improved. Other ideas to cover up the first line, or rub out the mention of the Jews (or "Juwes") were ignored. Warren erased the words, destroying vital evidence.

Warren resigned on 8th November 1888, the day before Mary Jane Kelly's body was found. Many assumed that the fifth victim of the Ripper was the cause, but in fact Warren had breached accepted procedure by writing an article responding to press attacks in *Murray's Magazine* without permission from the Home Office's Henry Matthews.

SIR ROBERT ANDERSON (1841-1918)

Sir Robert Anderson was appointed Assistant Commissioner of the Metropolitan CID on 1st September 1888. Jack the Ripper had already struck, killing his first victim, Mary Ann Nichols, on Friday 31st August, and it was to prove a baptism of fire for the new Assistant Commissioner. Anderson was due to take two or three months' sick leave from his post immediately, due to overwork, but it was recommended that he should defer the beginning of his leave a week until the 8th September. Anderson complied and travelled to Switzerland to recuperate. Unfortunately for him, bad timing meant that he left the country on the same day as the murder of Jack the Ripper's second victim, Annie Chapman.

Anderson received criticism for this unfortunate chain of events, which was beyond his control. However, he returned from his convalescence straight after the double murder – of Elizabeth Stride and Catherine Eddowes – which took place on 30th September 1888. Anderson recalled in *The Lighter Side of My Official Life* (his memoirs) reviewing files on the Ripper case as soon as he got back to England, then meeting with Sir Charles Warren and Henry Matthews, the Home Secretary. When discussing the Whitechapel murderer, Anderson promised that he would "take all legitimate means to find him".

The Metropolitan Police issued the following well-known 'Police Notice – To the Occupier' handbill, delivered to households in the East End:

'On the mornings of Friday, 31st August, Saturday 8th, and Sunday 30th September, 1888, women were murdered in or near Whitechapel, supposedly by some one residing in the immediate neighbourhood. Should you know of any person to whom suspicion is attached, you are earnestly requested to communicate at once with the nearest Police Station.'

Anderson distanced himself from the unpopular house-to-house investigation that followed the delivery of the handbills, beginning in early October. He stated incorrectly that he was still abroad, when he had actually returned to resume the murder investigations.

Sir Robert Anderson was unable to bring about the arrest of Jack the Ripper.

seased [...]
by us with difficulty. On orders [...]
him to identification, and he [...]
he was identified. On suspect [...]
At his brother's house in Whit [...]
he was watched by police (City [...]
day tonight. In a very short ti [...]
suspect with his hands tied [...]
his back, he was sent to Step [...]
workhouse and then to Colne [...]
and died shortly Afterwar [...]

Kosminski was the suspect

D.S.S.

In the famous 'Swanson marginalia', the Chief Inspector
identifies "Kosminski" as Anderson's suspect.

CHIEF INSPECTOR DONALD SUTHERLAND SWANSON (1848-1924)

Chief Inspector Donald Swanson was a highly-regarded police officer of his time, described as "one of the best class of officers" by colleague John Sweeney. In Sir Robert Anderson's absence due to sick leave during September 1888, Swanson was put in charge of the Whitechapel murders investigation by Sir Charles Warren (from 1st September until 6th October 1888). He took several statements from key suspects during police inquiries, including the logical investigations of those connected with the slaughter of animals: "Seventy six Butchers & Slaughterers have been visited & the characters of the men employed enquired into, this embraces all servants who had been employed for the past six months." On Anderson's return, Swanson liaised between the Assistant Commissioner and the detectives on the ground.

Swanson's importance in the Ripper case has only truly been acknowledged since the publication of the so-called 'Swanson marginalia' in 1987. Swanson remained friends with Anderson, who gave Swanson a copy of his memoirs, *The Lighter Side of My Official Life,* before they were published in 1910. Anderson had a definite suspect in mind as Jack the Ripper, but he refused to name him, only describing him as a poor Polish Jew from Whitechapel. He continued, "the only person who had ever had a good view of the murderer unhesitatingly identified the suspect the instant he was confronted with him; but he refused to give evidence against him." At this point in the 'Swanson marginalia' copy, in handwritten notes, Swanson added, "because the suspect was also a Jew and also because his evidence would convict the suspect, and witness would be the means of murderer being hanged, which he did not wish to be left on his mind. D.S.S."

Notes in the margin read, "And after this identification which suspect knew, no other murder of this kind took place in London." The endpapers of the book identify "Kosminski" as the suspect.

INSPECTOR FREDERICK GEORGE ABBERLINE (1843-1929)

After the murder of Jack the Ripper's first victim, Mary Ann Nichols, Inspector Frederick Abberline was sent from Scotland Yard to co-ordinate the police's divisional investigations. Surprisingly little is known about the lead detective in the Jack the Ripper case, although by all accounts he was a dedicated, efficient inspector with an extensive knowledge of East End criminals. In his autobiography, contemporary Walter Dew described Abberline's "abilities as a criminal hunter". Abberline worked very long hours, studying the case and writing up reports. He often wandered the "Abyss" of Whitechapel until four or five in the morning, "while keeping my eyes wide open for clues of any kind, have many and many a time given those wretched, homeless women, who were Jack the Ripper's special prey, fourpence or sixpence for a shelter to get them away from the streets and out of harm's way."

After the series of Whitechapel murders, Abberline was reported in *Cassell's Saturday Journal* of May 1892 as stating, "Theories! We were almost lost in them; there were so many of them." We can hear the lead detective's palpable frustration, years after the last Ripper killing. However, the article continued that Abberline had a new theory, "He believes from the evidence of his own eyesight that the Miller's Court atrocity was the last of the real series... and that in Miller's Court the murderer reached the culminating point of gratification of his morbid ideas."

Just over 10 years later, Abberline made it known that he believed that the Ripper was Severin Klosowski, also known as George Chapman. Abberline was convinced that the series of murders in Whitechapel ended, not because Jack the Ripper was dead, or locked up as a lunatic, as many believed, but because he had fled to America, where similar murders began to take place.

Johnny Depp starred as Inspector Frederick Abberline
in the film *From Hell* (2001).

Macnaghten, Assistant Commissioner of CID, named three suspects in his memoranda.
Montague John Druitt (bottom left) was named as his first suspect, Kominski, a Polish jew
as his second suspect and Michael Ostrog (bottom right) was his final suspect.

SIR MELVILLE LESLIE MACNAGHTEN (1853-1921)

Melville Macnaghten was offered the position of Assistant Chief Constable in 1887 by the Assistant Commissioner of CID, James Monro, but the move was vetoed by Sir Charles Warren. Macnaghten had to wait until after the Ripper murders to become personally involved in the case.

The main reason Melville Macnaghten is found to have such a prominent part in the Jack the Ripper case is his famous document, the *Macnaghten memoranda*, written on 23rd February 1894. Macnaghten felt moved to refute allegations in the *Sun* that suspect Thomas Cutbush was Jack the Ripper. He put forward a case for three suspects that were "more likely than Cutbush to have committed this series of murders". In addition, Macnaghten stated categorically that he believed that the "Whitechapel murderer had 5 victims – & 5 victims only".

Macnaghten's three proposed suspects were:
"1/ A Mr. M.J. Druitt, said to be a doctor & of good family, who disappeared at the time of the Miller's Court murder, whose body (which was said to have been upwards of a month in the water) was found in the Thames on 31st December – or about seven weeks after the murder. He was sexually insane and from private info I have little doubt but that his own family believed him to be the murderer.

2/ Kosminski, a Polish Jew, & resident in Whitechapel. This man became insane owing to many years' indulgence in solitary vices. He had a great hatred of women, specially of the prostitute class, & had strong homicidal tendencies; he was removed to a lunatic asylum about March 1889. There were many circs [circumstances] connected with this man which made him a strong 'suspect'.

3/ Michael Ostrog, a Russian doctor, and a convict, who was subsequently detained in a lunatic asylum as a homicidal maniac. This man's antecedents were of the worst possible type, and his whereabouts at the time of the murders could never be ascertained."

SERGEANT WILLIAM THICK
(1845-1930)

Based in Whitechapel during the Autumn of Terror, Sergeant William Thick, along with Inspectors Moore, Nairn and Reid and Sergeants McCarthy and Pearce, reported to Chief Inspector Frederick Abberline. Sergeant Thick was a well-regarded, experienced detective spending much of his working career with H Division. He became involved in the Whitechapel murder investigations, but was also named as a suspect himself in 1889. Thick, also referred to as Thicke on occasion, had good knowledge of many of the criminals in the East End.

American writer Jack London (1876-1916), author of *White Fang* and *Call of the Wild* also wrote *The People of the Abyss* published in 1903, documenting the awful social conditions of much of Whitechapel. London met Sergeant Thick, describing him as "shades of old sleuth and Sherlock Holmes". He called him 'Johnny Upright', a nickname that Walter Dew explained came from Sergeant Thick's upright bearing as well as his honest police methods. Dew further described him as "an unholy terror to local lawbreakers".

Early in the murder investigations, following the suspicions around an elusive character named 'Leather Apron', Thick arrested John Pizer at 22 Mulberry Street. Timothy Donovan, the lodging house keeper of second Ripper victim Annie Chapman, mentioned to police that he had thrown Pizer out of his lodging house for attacking a woman – and that he had seen Pizer wearing a deerstalker hat (said to be worn by Annie Chapman's killer). Thick made a search of 22 Mulberry Street, unearthing several long-bladed knives.

At the inquest of second victim Annie Chapman, Sergeant William Thick gave evidence. He recounted that he had known Pizer for several years and that in the local Whitechapel area, if anyone mentioned 'Leather Apron' they meant John Pizer.

Punch satirised the police's attempts to catch
Jack the Ripper on 22nd September 1888.

Walter Dew was unfortunate enough to see the corpse of Mary Jane Kelly.

DETECTIVE WALTER DEW (1863-1947)

Walter Dew was a detective constable in H Division during the time of the Whitechapel murders. Soon after the murder of second victim Annie Chapman in Hanbury Street, Dew was standing in the same street when he noticed 'Squibby' – a violent criminal. Squibby was known to have thrown a brick at a police officer, but missed and hit a child. Dew went to arrest the villain, who ran off. Dew gave chase, but so too did a mob of bloodthirsty locals, mistakenly believing that Squibby was the Whitechapel murderer. It must have been a frightening scene, not only for Squibby, but also for Dew, who had to try to control the angry rabble. It took several hours for the crowd to calm down.

A more horrific encounter took place on Friday 9th October 1888. Shortly before 11.00am, Thomas Bowyer, rent collector for John McCarthy on Dorset Street, arrived in a hurry at Commercial Street police station, where Walter Dew was working. The young man was in a state, but managed to say, "Another one. Jack the Ripper. Awful." The staccato message was enough to convey the necessary details to Walter Dew and Inspector Walter Beck. They followed Bowyer straight back to 13 Miller's Court, off Dorset Street.

They were told that the key to number 13 had been lost by the tenants so the door remained closed. Beck drew away the curtain from a broken window and witnessed the carnage of Mary Jane Kelly's corpse inside. He told Walter Dew not to look. As a thorough detective with natural curiosity, Dew did look. He saw something that he would never be able to forget.

'Blue Serge', as Walter Dew was nicknamed, became a chief inspector in 1906. In 1910, Dew was involved in the transatlantic pursuit of murderer Dr. Hawley Harvey Crippen. Dew became a hero due to the well-publicised capture of Dr. Crippen.

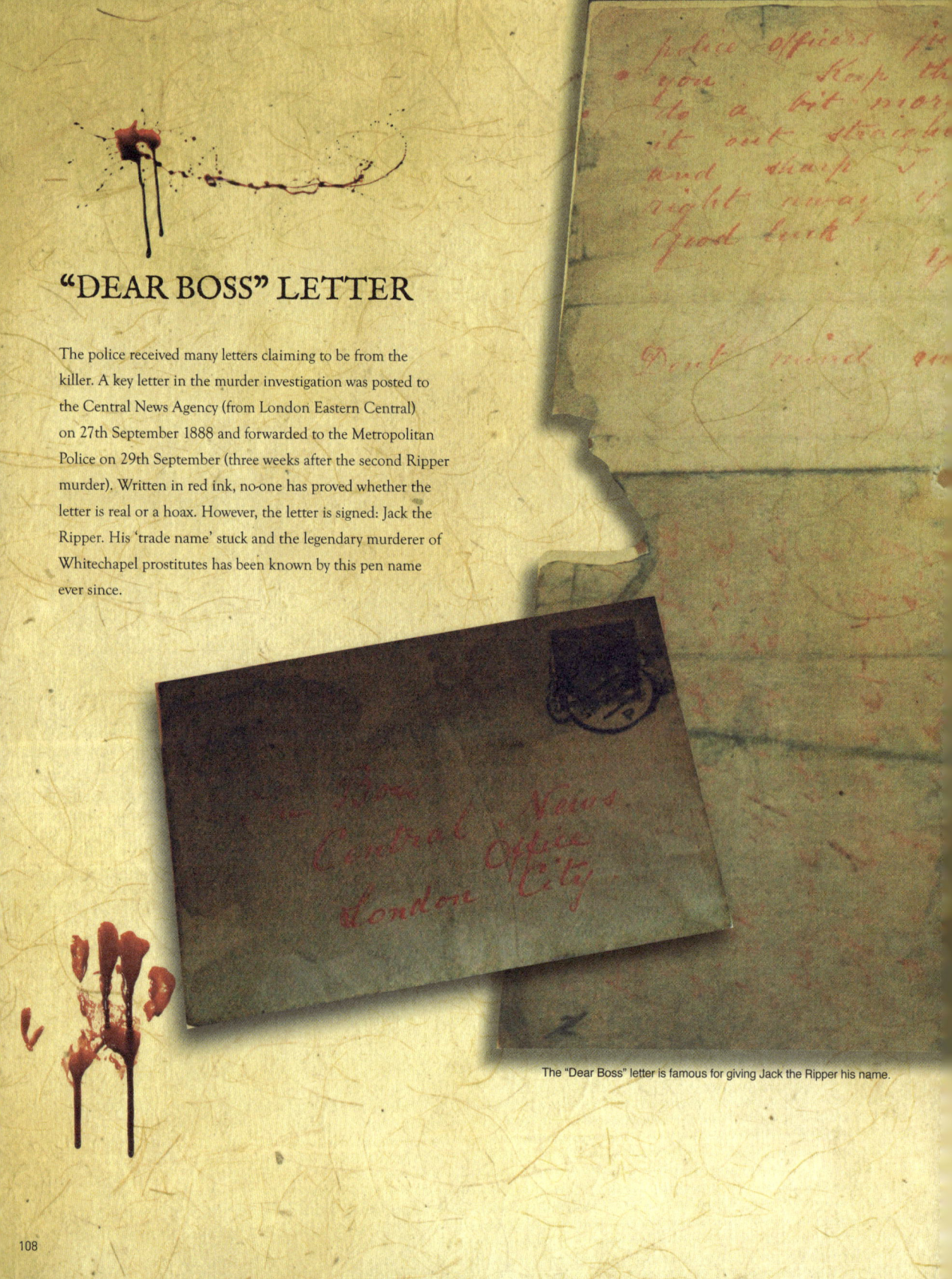

"DEAR BOSS" LETTER

The police received many letters claiming to be from the
killer. A key letter in the murder investigation was posted to
the Central News Agency (from London Eastern Central)
on 27th September 1888 and forwarded to the Metropolitan
Police on 29th September (three weeks after the second Ripper
murder). Written in red ink, no-one has proved whether the
letter is real or a hoax. However, the letter is signed: Jack the
Ripper. His 'trade name' stuck and the legendary murderer of
Whitechapel prostitutes has been known by this pen name
ever since.

The "Dear Boss" letter is famous for giving Jack the Ripper his name.

25TH SEPT. 1988.

DEAR BOSS

I KEEP ON HEARING THE POLICE HAVE CAUGHT ME BUT THEY WONT FIX ME
JUST YET. I HAVE LAUGHED WHEN THEY LOOK SO CLEVER AND TALK ABOUT
BEING ON THE RIGHT TRACK. THAT JOKE ABOUT LEATHER APRON GAVE ME
REAL FITS.

I AM DOWN ON WHORES AND I SHANT QUIT RIPPING THEM TILL I DO GET
BUCKLED. GRAND WORK THE LAST JOB WAS. I GAVE THE LADY NO TIME TO
SQUEAL. HOW CAN THEY CATCH ME NOW? I LOVE MY WORK AND WANT TO
START AGAIN. YOU WILL SOON HEAR OF ME WITH MY FUNNY LITTLE GAMES.
I SAVED SOME OF THE PROPER RED STUFF IN A GINGER BEER BOTTLE OVER
THE LAST JOB TO WRITE WITH BUT IT WENT THICK LIKE GLUE AND I CANT USE
IT. RED INK IS FIT ENOUGH I HOPE <u>HA. HA.</u> THE NEXT JOB I DO I SHALL CLIP
THE LADYS EARS OFF AND SEND TO THE POLICE OFFICERS JUST FOR JOLLY
WOULDN'T YOU.

KEEP THIS LETTER BACK TILL I DO A BIT MORE WORK, THEN GIVE IT OUT
STRAIGHT. MY KNIFE'S SO NICE AND SHARP I WANT TO GET TO WORK RIGHT
AWAY IF I GET THE CHANCE.

GOOD LUCK.

YOURS TRULY

JACK THE RIPPER

DON'T MIND ME GIVING THE TRADE NAME

The above section was written by a well-educated hand, visible
in the neat handwriting, known as 'copperplate'. A second
postscript appears to have been added in red crayon, rather
than ink:

WASN'T GOOD ENOUGH TO POST THIS BEFORE I GOT ALL THE RED INK OFF MY
HANDS CURSE IT

No LUCK YET. THEY SAY I'M A DOCTOR NOW <u>HA HA</u>

WHITECHAPEL, 1888.

The police were under immense pressure
during the time of the Whitechapel murders.

'SAUCY JACK' POSTCARD

The 'Saucy Jacky' postcard was posted to the Central News Agency on the 1st October. It seemed to be similar handwriting to the earlier 'Dear Boss' letter, although it appeared in a slightly rougher and more hurried style. Bloody fingerprints (or more likely, smeary prints made from red ink) cover both the address on the front of the postcard and the writing on the back, making some of the words difficult to read.

I WAS NOT CODDING

DEAR OLD BOSS WHEN

I GAVE YOU THE TIP

YOU'LL HEAR ABOUT

SAUCY JACKYS WORK

TOMORROW DOUBLE

EVENT THIS TIME

NUMBER ONE SQUEALED

A BIT COULDN'T

FINISH STRAIGHT

OFF. HAD NOT TIME

TO GET EARS FOR

POLICE THANKS FOR

KEEPING LAST LETTER

BACK TILL I GOT

TO WORK AGAIN.

JACK THE RIPPER

The writer addresses the recipient 'Boss' once more, linking the postcard to the 'Dear Boss' letter. He also refers to: 1. "keeping last letter back" (which he had requested in the earlier letter) and 2. "had not time to get ears" (a further reference to the 'Dear Boss' letter, which promised: "The next job I do I shall clip the ladys ears off and send to the police officers just for jolly").

Despite referring to the "tomorrow double event", the postcard proves nothing. The double murder, which takes place on Sunday September 30th, predates the 'Saucy Jacky' postcard, which has a postmark from the day after the murders, on Monday the 1st October.

LETTER 'FROM HELL'

The 'From Hell' letter was received in the post on 16th October 1888 by George Akin Lusk, and is also referred to as the 'Lusk Letter'. George Lusk was President and Chairman of the recently-formed Whitechapel Vigilance Committee, set up by local residents to assist the police in their hunt for the murderer.

Accompanying the letter was a piece of human kidney, which the writer refers to ("half the Kidne"). He is suggesting that this kidney belongs to the Mitre Square victim, Catherine Eddowes.

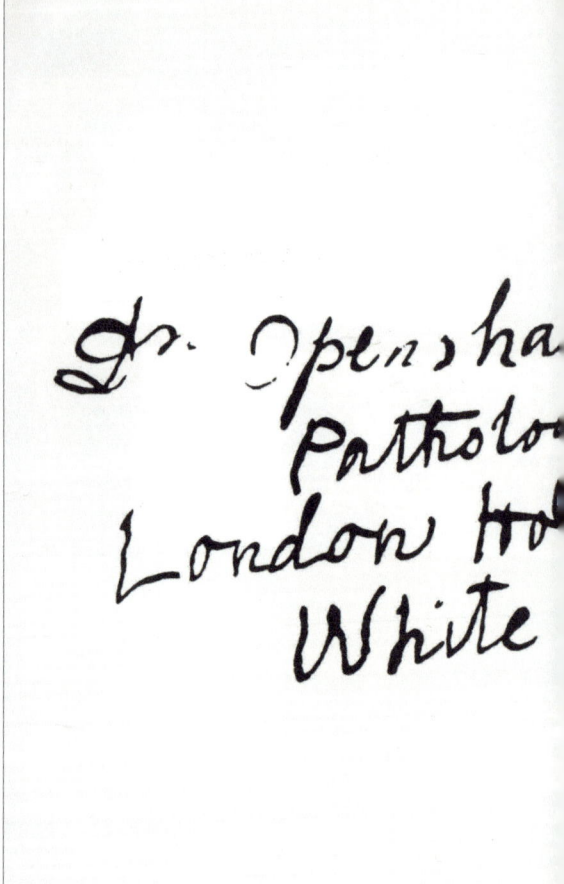

FROM HELL

MR. LUSK

SOR

I SEND YOU HALF THE KIDNE I TOOK FROM ONE WOMEN PRASARVED IT FOR YOU TOTHER PIECE I FRIED AND ATE IT WAS VERY NISE I MAY SEND YOU THE BLOODY KNIF THAT TOOK IT OUT IF YOU ONLY WATE A WHIL LONGER

SIGNED

CATCH ME WHEN

YOU CAN

MISHTER LUSK.

George Lusk believed this to be a stunt, but was persuaded to send the kidney to Dr. Thomas Horrocks Openshaw of the London Hospital for analysis. He was misquoted in the press as calling it a woman's 'ginny' kidney, preserved in spirits of wine. Further examinations of the kidney have been inconclusive, but most believe that the letter and the kidney were part of a hoax.

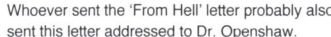

Whoever sent the 'From Hell' letter probably also sent this letter addressed to Dr. Openshaw.

A further letter, from the same hand, was sent to Dr. Openshaw on 29th October 1888:

OLD BOSS YOU WAS RITE IT WAS
THE LEFT KIDNEY I WOS GOIN TO
HOPPERATE AGIN CLOSE TO YOUR
OSPITLE JUST AS I WAS GOIN
TO DROR MI NIFE ALONG OF
ER BLOOMIN THROTE THEM
CUSSES OF COPPERS SPOILT
THE GAME BUT I GUESS I WIL
BE ON THE JOB SOON AND WILL
SEND YOU ANOTHER BIT OF
INNERDS

JACK THE RIPPER

O HAVE YOU SEEN THE DELVE
WITH HIS MIKERSCOPE AND SCALPEL
A LOOKIN AT A KIDNEY
WITH A SLIDE COCKED UP.

17th SEPTEMBER LETTER

From '17th Sept. 1888', the letter purports to come from a time between the murder of Annie Chapman (on 8th September 1888) and the date of the double murder of Elizabeth Stride and Catherine Eddowes (on 30th September 1888). Signed "Jack the Ripper", the letter was found in the National Archives in 1988 by Peter McClelland.

17TH SEPT. 1888

DEAR BOSS

SO NOW THAY SAY I
AM A YID WHEN WILL THAY
LERN DEAR OLD BOSS? YOU AN
ME KNOW THE TRUTH DONT WE.
LUSK CAN LOOK FOREVER HELL
NEVER FIND ME BUT I AM RITE
UNDER HIS NOSE ALL THE TIME.
I WATCH THEM LOOKING FOR ME
AN IT GIVES ME FITS HA HA. I
LOVE MY WORK AN I SHANT STOP
UNTIL I GET BUCKLED AND EVEN
THEN WATCH OUT FOR YOUR OLD
PAL JACKY

CATCH ME IF YOU CAN

JACK THE RIPPER
SORRY ABOUT THE BLOOD STILL
MESSY FROM THE LAST ONE. WHAT
A PRETTY NECKLACE I GAVE HER

The Ripper caught red-handed: this was wishful thinking.

THE ORDONAPEY MURDER   THE CRY IS JACK THE RIPPER

The capital letters are much larger and more ornate, and the hand overall appears different to other Jack the Ripper correspondence. Many words and phrases reappear lifted directly from earlier Ripper letters, for example: "Dear Boss", "Dear old Boss", "ha ha", "get buckled", "fits", "Jacky" and "Catch me if you can". The result is that this piece of writing seems to be an attempt to recreate a contemporary Jack the Ripper letter. In other words, it appears to be a modern forgery – and not a very sophisticated hoax at that.

THE SERIAL KILLER

WHAT IS A SERIAL KILLER?

The term 'serial killer' is one with which we are now familiar.
The phenomenon is not a new one, but the term itself is recent,
and did not exist 50 years ago. Federal Bureau of Investigation
agent and member of the FBI psychological profiling team
Robert Ressler is often credited for coining the term 'serial
killer' in the 1970s – to describe those that murder several
victims, obsessively, and often with a sexual motive. Before
then, a killer who murdered in this way was known as a 'mass
murderer'. The more recent term 'serial killer' is a useful one,
and seems clearer.

Nowadays a 'serial killer' is generally defined to be someone
who kills three or more people, one at a time, over a relatively
short period. Jack the Ripper was an early example of the
serial killer. He was not a prolific killer: he is thought to have
murdered five victims, more or less. Many other British serial
killers have murdered more. These notorious criminals are,
unfortunately, household names, for example, Peter Sutcliffe,
Dennis Nilsen, Harold Shipman, and the serial-killing couple,
Fred and Rose West.

Peter Sutcliffe, usually attacking his victims from behind with
a hammer, killed 13, but attempted to murder a further seven.
Carrying out his attacks and murders in the north of England
between 1975 and 1981, he is better known as the 'Yorkshire
Ripper'. Dennis Nilsen, 'the Kindly Killer', murdered 15 young
men between 1978 and 1983. Fred West, with his wife Rose,
killed at least 12, but before committing suicide in 1995, he
admitted there were more. Harold Shipman, also known as
'Doctor Death', murdered his patients – probably in excess
of 250, from 1975 to 1998.

Serial killers fascinate and repel. We seek to understand how,
and why, these chilling psychopathic personalities could do
such things. But in many ways they are very ordinary people.
The Byford report in 1981 described Peter Sutcliffe as "an
otherwise unremarkable young man".

The police issued this photofit image in 1979 for the so-called 'Yorkshire Ripper'. Serial killer Peter Sutcliffe was caught in January 1981.

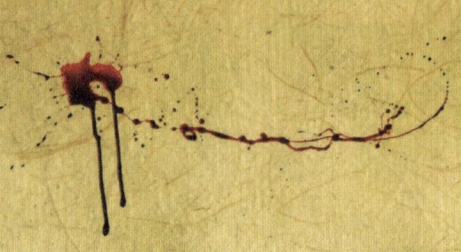

PROFILING JACK THE RIPPER

If they have psychopathic personalities, serial killers commit murder but their mental disorder is such that they may not feel any remorse about these acts. These callous killers are pathological liars, but can also exhibit great charm, as well as cunning and manipulation – if that helps them achieve their goal at the time. The normal, human ability to experience empathy – putting yourself in someone else's shoes – is curiously lacking. Or, as recent research seems to demonstrate, psychopaths are able to switch empathy on at will.

In 1988, John Douglas and Roy Hazelwood of the FBI prepared a psychological profile, made for the television documentary *The Secret Identity of Jack the Ripper*. Having studied the murders, they concluded the following features of the profile:

- Local, resident male in his late 20s
- Probably employed (murders generally occurred at the weekends)
- Single, without family ties (murders took place between 12.00am and 6.00am)
- Of low class (murders showed lack of care/attention to detail)
- Not surgically skilled or possessing anatomical knowledge
- Probably known to the police
- Seen by acquaintances as a loner
- Probably abused/deserted as a child by his mother

Douglas and Hazelwood's psychological profile of Jack the Ripper suggested he was a local resident, known to police and likely to be a loner.

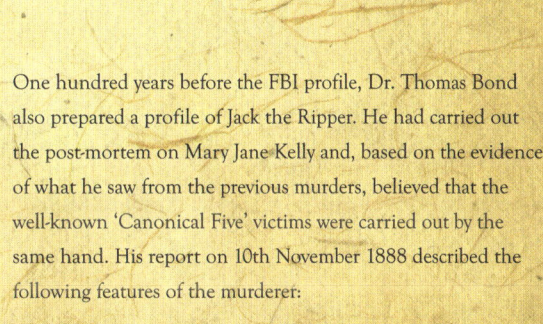

One hundred years before the FBI profile, Dr. Thomas Bond also prepared a profile of Jack the Ripper. He had carried out the post-mortem on Mary Jane Kelly and, based on the evidence of what he saw from the previous murders, believed that the well-known 'Canonical Five' victims were carried out by the same hand. His report on 10th November 1888 described the following features of the murderer:

- Probably middle-aged
- Probably not in regular employment
- Physically strong
- Quiet and inoffensive in appearance; neatly and respectably dressed
- Probably lacking anatomical knowledge
- Probably solitary
- Probably eccentric in behaviour

It is perhaps unsurprising to find differences in the profiling from 1888 and 1988. At the same time certain features – in the perception of what sort of person Jack the Ripper was – have remained the same.

THE SUSPECTS

'LEATHER APRON' AKA JOHN PIZER (1850-1897)

After the murder of Mary Ann Nichols, many people wanted a scapegoat. Inventing suspects fulfilled a need, for both the police and the public, when there was a lack of genuine evidence. One suspect known as 'Leather Apron', who regularly terrorised prostitutes, came to light. The *Star* newspaper began a crusade to warn the public of the danger of Leather Apron: "His eyes glinted, his smile was repulsive and he wore a close-fitting cap and a leather apron. He walked soundlessly, carried a knife and frequently threatened, 'I'll rip you up!'" One major feature of the suspect was his Jewish appearance, as this was at a time when anti-Semitism was growing in the East End.

The *Daily News* reported with a note of caution that, "The public are looking for a monster, and in the legend of Leather Apron, the Whitechapel part of them seem to be inventing a monster to look for. This kind of invention ought to be discouraged in every possible way, or there may soon be murders from panic to add to murders from lust of blood."

At the second murder scene – of Annie Chapman at 29 Hanbury Street – a leather apron was found. However, this "clue" belonged to John Richardson, the son of Amelia Richardson who owned the packing-case business on the premises. A police report on 7th September 1888 identified Leather Apron as John Pizer, a Jewish shoemaker. Pizer, having previously been pursued by a "howling crowd", had gone into hiding at his brother's home at 22 Mulberry Street. On 10th September, Sergeant Thick arrived at the same address, arresting Pizer: "You are just the man I'm looking for." John Pizer was accused of the Whitechapel murders, but was able to account for his movements on the night of Mary Ann Nichols' death and was acquitted.

GHASTLY
MURDER
IN THE EAST-END.
DREADFUL MUTILATION OF A WOMAN.

Capture : Leather Apron

Another murder of a character even more diabolical than that perpetrated in Buck's Row, on Friday week, was discovered in the same neighbourhood, on Saturday morning. At about six o'clock a woman was found lying in a back yard at the foot of a passage leading to a lodging-house in a Old Brown's Lane, Spitalfields. The house is occupied by a Mrs. Richardson, who lets it out to lodgers, and the door which admits to this passage, at the foot of which lies the yard where the body was found, is always open for the convenience of lodgers. A lodger named Davis was going down to work at the time mentioned and found the woman lying on her back close to the flight of steps leading into the yard. Her throat was cut in a fearful manner. The woman's body had been completely ripped open, and the heart and other organs laying about the place, and portions of the entrails round the victim's neck. An excited crowd gathered in front of Mrs. Richardson's house and also round the mortuary in old Montague Street, whither the body was quickly conveyed. As the body lies in the rough coffin in which it has been placed in the mortuary —the same coffin in which the unfortunate Mrs. Nicholls was first placed—it presents a fearful sight. The body is that of a woman about 45 years of age. The hair is slightly five feet. The complexion is fair, with wavy dark brown hair; the eyes are brown lower teeth have been knocked out. The nose is rather large and prom

According to the *New York Times*, early suspect Leather Apron had "small, wicked black eyes and is half crazy". Initially, John Pizer (right) was thought to be Leather Apron.

125

Thomas Cutbush fitted the description
of a mad, dangerous attacker.

THOMAS HAYNE CUTBUSH (1865-1903)

On 13th February 1894, the *Sun* newspaper began to publish a series of articles called *The Story of Jack the Ripper: Solution of the great murder mystery* in which it proposed a suspect. He was not named, but it was clear from the articles that the identity was Thomas Hayne Cutbush, who had been sent to Broadmoor Criminal Lunatic Asylum in April 1891.

Prior to his committal to Broadmoor, Cutbush had been detained at Lambeth Infirmary. He escaped, however, and stabbed Florence Grace Johnson in the buttocks. Cutbush was also linked with attacks in south London in early 1891 of five other young women, who were stabbed in the back or rear. The *Sun* believed that, on this evidence, Cutbush was Jack the Ripper. Medical records from Broadmoor reveal, "On 24th April 1891 he was described as having a vacant expression and protruding eyes. He was restless and incoherent." While Cutbush was violent and insane, he was not Jack the Ripper.

The significance of Cutbush to the Jack the Ripper case should not be underestimated. As a result of the implication of Cutbush as the murderer, Sir Melville Macnaghten wrote a document now known as the *Macnaghten memoranda*, in which he refuted the validity of the articles in the *Sun* newspaper: "It will be noticed that the fury of the [Ripper] mutilations *increased* in each case, and, seemingly, the appetite only became sharpened by indulgence. It seems, then, highly improbable that the murderer would have suddenly stopped in November '88, and been content to recommence operations by merely prodding a girl's behind some 2 years and 4 months afterwards." Macnaghten went on to name three suspects that he believed were "more likely than Cutbush to have committed this series of murders". They were Druitt, Kosminski and Ostrog.

MONTAGUE JOHN DRUITT (1857-1888)

When Sir Melville Macnaghten referred to three more likely suspects than Thomas Cutbush, the first name on his list was Montague John Druitt. A well-to-do barrister with chambers on King's Bench Walk in the Inner Temple, Druitt was also an assistant schoolmaster at a boarding school in Blackheath. On 30th November 1888 he was dismissed as a teacher for what was recorded as "serious trouble". A month later his body was found floating in the River Thames at Chiswick. His brother, William, discovered a letter revealing his tormented mind, which read as follows: "Since Friday I felt I was going to be like mother, and the best thing for me was to die." At his inquest, it was revealed that his mother had gone insane the previous year.

Connecting Montague John Druitt with the Jack the Ripper murders, Macnaghten recounted that Druitt "disappeared at the time of the Miller's Court murder" and that "he was sexually insane and from private info I have little doubt but that his own family believed him to have been the murderer." Macnaghten does not specify what "private info" he has, but this is not compelling evidence.

Macnaghten speculated that "the murderer's brain gave way altogether after his awful glut in Miller's Court, and that he immediately committed suicide, or, as a possible alternative, was found to be so hopelessly mad by his relations, that he was by them confined in some asylum." Druitt would, therefore, have fitted Macnaghten's own preferred theory of an insane Jack the Ripper committing suicide. There has to be a reason for the sudden end to the killings and this theory would offer a neat explanation. The problem is that Druitt continued working for a further three weeks at the Bar and the boarding school, until his dismissal on the 30th November. It is more likely that the shame of his dismissal drove him to suicide.

If Montague Druitt was Jack the Ripper, the date of his suicide matched the end of the killing spree in Whitechapel in November 1888.

The "Autumn of Terror" provided a shortage of genuine suspects: Polish Jew Kosminski was seen as one of the more likely, having been sent to an asylum in early 1889.

KOSMINSKI (1865-1919)

The second suspect on *Macnaghten's memoranda* list is Kosminski. According to the Scotland Yard version of the notes, Kosminski was a 'Polish Jew, & resident in Whitechapel'. A second version, known as Lady Aberconway's copy, has a slightly longer résumé of the suspect: "Kosminski, a Polish Jew, who lived in the very heart of the district where the murders were committed. He had become insane owing to many years indulgence in solitary vices. He had a great hatred of women, with strong homicidal tendencies. He was (and still is) detained in a lunatic asylum about March 1889. This man in appearance strongly resembled the individual seen by the City PC near Mitre Square."

In addition to Macnaghten's proposition of Kosminski as a suspect, the two highest-ranking police officers with direct responsibility for the murder investigations – Sir Robert Anderson and Chief Inspector Donald Swanson – both believed that Kosminski was Jack the Ripper. Anderson wrote in *The Lighter Side of My Official Life* memoirs that, "in saying that he was a Polish Jew I am merely stating a definitely ascertained fact." Swanson wrote pencil notes in his own personal copy of Anderson's memoirs (his 'Marginalia'), adding that the suspect was taken to Colney Hatch Asylum – and that "Kosminski was the suspect".

Investigation into Colney Hatch Asylum archives by prominent Ripperologists Martin Fido and Philip Sugden reveal that Kosminski was most likely Aaron Kosminski (1865–1919), a paranoid schizophrenic. Although Swanson believed that the suspect died shortly after entering Colney Hatch, Aaron Kosminski transferred to Leavesden Asylum near Watford, where he died in 1919. Apart from one occasion at Colney Hatch, when he picked up a chair and attempted to strike the charge attendant, Kosminski was not seen to be a danger to others.

MICHAEL OSTROG (BORN C.1833)

Sir Melville Macnaghten's third and final suspect on his list contained within the memoranda was Michael Ostrog. Macnaghten seems to know little about Ostrog, but described him as a "Russian doctor, and a convict who was subsequently detained in a lunatic asylum as a homicidal maniac". It is certain, however, that Ostrog was a thief and a swindler, who had countless aliases, which he used to cover his tracks as he toured around Britain. His other identities included Bertrand Ashley (aka Ashley Nabokoff, "the great Russian swindler"), Max Grief Gosslar, Dr. Grant, Stanislas Lublinski, Henry Ray and Count Sobieski (the exiled son of the King of Poland).

The Aberconway version of the Macnaghten memoranda is more expansive about Michael Ostrog: "This man was said to have been habitually cruel to women, and for a long time was known to have carried about with him surgical knives and other instruments; his antecedents [previous convictions] were of the very worst and his whereabouts at the time of the Whitechapel murders could never be satisfactorily accounted for. He is still alive."

In October 1888, as the Jack the Ripper investigations reached fever pitch, Ostrog was, according to the *Police Gazette,* wanted for failure to report to the police. The article warned, "Special attention is called to this dangerous man." Ostrog's failure to report to the police – and his whereabouts at the time of the Whitechapel murders – can be explained. After yet another misdemeanour under a different alias, Ostrog was being held in custody in France from the end of July to the middle of November 1888 – thus ruling him out as a suspect for all five Jack the Ripper murders.

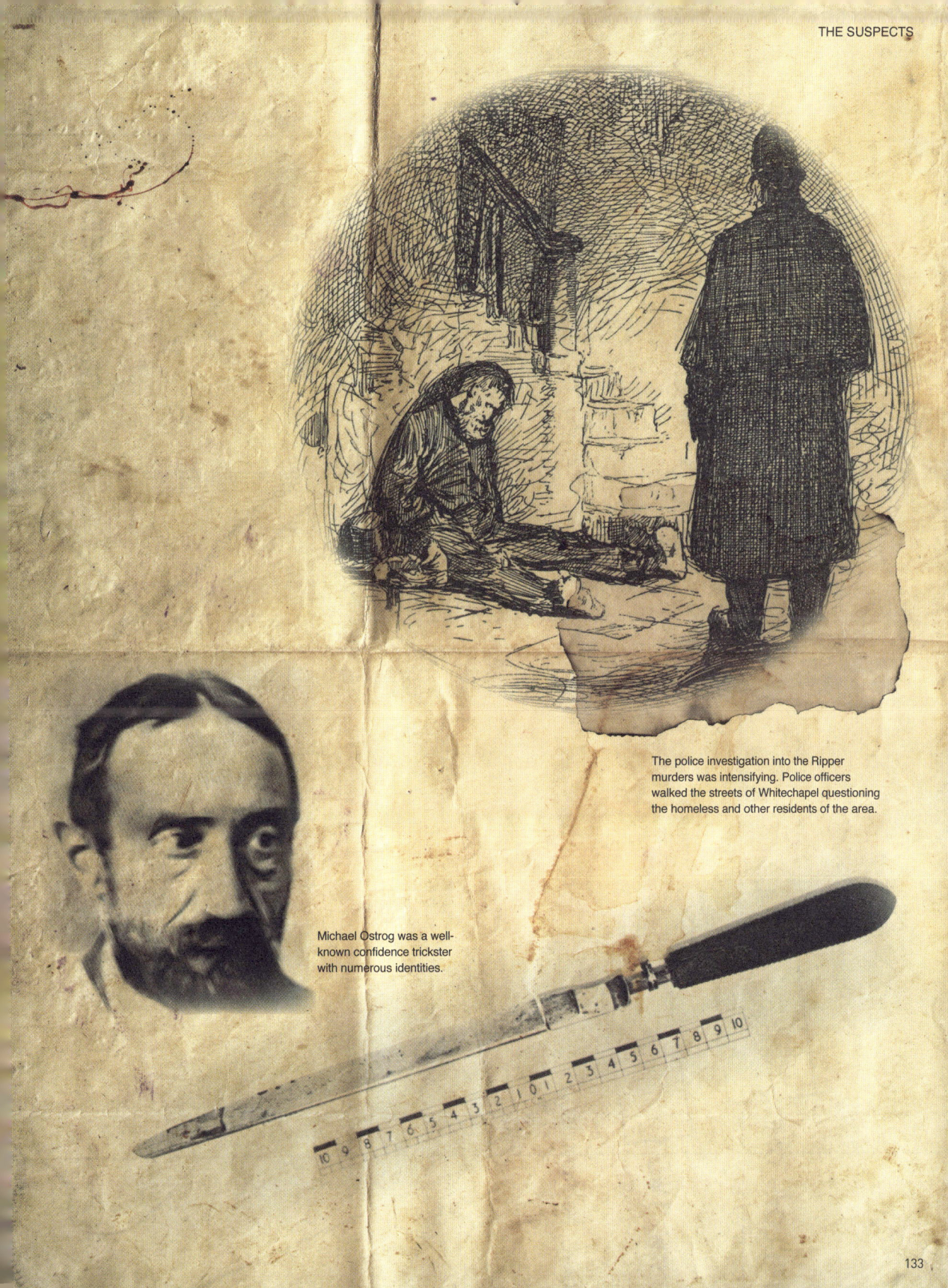

The police investigation into the Ripper murders was intensifying. Police officers walked the streets of Whitechapel questioning the homeless and other residents of the area.

Michael Ostrog was a well-known confidence trickster with numerous identities.

Polish-born George Chapman was Abberline's favoured suspect.

GEORGE CHAPMAN (1865-1903) AKA SEVERIN KLOSOWSKI

George Chapman was Inspector Frederick Abberline's preferred choice for the moniker of Jack the Ripper. Born in Poland on 14th December 1865, Severin Antoniovich Klosowski studied to be a junior surgeon, failed in his studies, and moved to London in 1887. He married Lucy Baderski in the summer of 1889 and worked as a hairdresser's assistant in Whitechapel High Street. By 1893, Klosowski had found a new woman called Annie Chapman (no relation to the Ripper's second victim), and from then on was known as George Chapman.

Thereafter, Chapman had a number of lovers and wives, all of whom expired soon after meeting him: Mary Spink died on 25th December 1897; Bessie Taylor died on 14th February 1901; and Maud Marsh died on 22nd October 1902. Chapman was arrested three days after the death of Maud Marsh, on suspicion of poisoning her. His trial in March 1903 lasted only four days and he was found guilty.

So why did Inspector Abberline think that George Chapman was Jack the Ripper? Abberline claimed that the connection had not occurred to him until the Attorney General made his opening statement at Chapman's trial. From then on, it appears Abberline becomes obsessed with this possibility, being unable to "think of anything else for several days" and realising that "there are a score of things which make one believe that Chapman is the man". The main reasons for Abberline's view were that Chapman had studied surgery (Jack the Ripper's skill as a "surgeon" has always been a matter of debate) and that he arrived in England at the start of the Whitechapel murders. Despite George Chapman murdering a number of women, his *modus operandi* is in stark contrast with that of Jack the Ripper. Would 'Saucy Jacky' really change from a knife-wielding maniac to a patient poisoner?

PRINCE ALBERT VICTOR CHRISTIAN EDWARD (1864-1892)

One name that persistently crops up among people suspected to be Jack the Ripper is a member of the royal family, Prince Albert Victor Christian Edward, more commonly known as Prince Eddy. Grandson of Queen Victoria, Prince Albert Victor was Duke of Clarence and Avondale from 1891.

The rumour that there was a royal connection to the crimes had been circulating, according to author Colin Wilson, for several years before Philippe Jullian published his *Edouard VII* in 1962. Jullian stated, "Before he died, poor Clarence was a great anxiety to his family... The young man's evil reputation soon spread. The rumour gained ground that he was Jack the Ripper..."

In his article *Jack the Ripper – A Solution?* in the *Criminologist* in 1970, Dr. Thomas Stowell identified 'Mr. S' as Jack the Ripper (apparently he had wanted to use the mysterious 'Mr. X', but was advised against it – the 'S' did not stand for anything). Although he later denied that 'S' was Prince Eddy, it was clear what Stowell was inferring. Stowell stated that 'S' had completely lost his mind due to syphilis, and having been detained after killing Catherine Eddowes, he had escaped – to kill Mary Jane Kelly.

Rather than Prince Eddy suffering a "softening of the brain", the theory itself bore all the hallmarks of feeble-mindedness. Buckingham Palace was quick to react to such suggestions, with the following statement, "The idea that Edward VII's eldest son and, but for his early death of pneumonia aged 28, heir to the throne, should have bestially murdered five or six women of 'unfortunate' class in the East End is regarded as too ridiculous for comment."

The royal statement went on to prove that Prince Albert Victor had been in Scotland at the time of the double murder (30th September) and at Sandringham in Norfolk at the time of Mary Jane Kelly's murder (9th November).

Prince Eddy was one of many famous public figures
to be connected with the Jack the Ripper murders.

Well-connected with royalty,
Sir William Withey Gull was
a suspect.

SIR WILLIAM WITHEY GULL
(1816-1890)

Another suspect with royal connections was Sir William Withey Gull. He was 'physician-in-ordinary' to Queen Victoria from 1887 to 1890. Even before becoming the Queen's surgeon, Gull was an eminent physician, identifying and naming the condition of anorexia nervosa.

Dr. Thomas Stowell, who also fingered Prince Albert Victor as a shady killer, identified Gull as a potential Ripper suspect. He mentioned the theories circulating that Jack the Ripper was a surgeon and that the royal physician had been spotted more than once in the Whitechapel area on the night of a murder. Despite these assertions, there have been no independent confirmations of either of these claims.

At the time of the Autumn of Terror caused by the Ripper attacks, Sir William Gull would have been more than 70 years old, and not in the rudest of health. The previous year he had suffered a minor stroke, which left him partially paralysed on his right side. Gull admitted to lapses of memory as a result of the stroke – and that once he had found blood on his shirt, without knowing how it got there. He went on to have three epileptic attacks and two further strokes, before dying in January 1890.

In Stephen Knight's account of *Jack the Ripper: The Final Solution* published in 1976, Sir William Withey Gull was to be connected once more with the murders of Jack the Ripper. The author went into great detail to support his case, which originated from a man called Joseph Sickert, that the eminent surgeon had carried out the murders to cover up an illegal marriage between Prince Albert Victor and Sickert's grandmother, Annie Elizabeth Cook.

ROBERT DONSTON STEPHENSON (1841-1916)

Robert Donston Stephenson called himself Dr. Rosyln D'Onston and told a colourful tale of his life that bore scant comparison with reality. Born in Hull in 1841, he studied chemistry in Munich and became interested in black magic. During the summer of 1888, the tall, fair-moustachioed Stephenson moved from Brighton and booked himself into the London Hospital on Whitechapel Road, suffering from neurasthenia (a nervous disorder characterised by crippling fatigue). Treatment for the disorder would entail rest in order to recover from stress. Some have argued that it was possible that he was in fact suffering from alcoholism.

Stephenson remained in hospital until 7th December 1888. However, the proximity of the hospital (situated on Whitechapel Road) to the murder sites in the East End make the fake doctor an interesting candidate for Jack the Ripper – if he was able to disappear from the hospital late at night, and return, without being detected or arousing suspicion. The first murder in Buck's Row (of Mary Ann Nichols) was a mere two or three minutes away. Records indicate, however, that Stephenson had a bed in the Currie Ward until at least the middle of October 1888, and patients in this section of the hospital were prevented from leaving the ward at night.

In an interesting twist, Stephenson wrote to the City police on the 16th October, a couple of weeks after the double murder, with a theory about the Goulston Street graffito. He suggested that the word 'Juwes' might indicate that a Frenchman wrote the message, if the word was in fact 'Juives' (the French for Jewish women). The following month, sharing a private ward with another patient, he observed Dr. Morgan Davies re-enact in a bizarre manner what he supposed was Jack the Ripper's method of disposing of Mary Jane Kelly. According to Stephenson, the doctor's over-excited behaviour proved that he was Jack the Ripper. Stephenson himself was an enigmatic character, a fantasist who drank and took drugs regularly, and he continues to be a suspect.

Suspect Robert Donston Stephenson was in the London Hospital on Whitechapel Road at the time of the murders.

Quack doctor Francis Tumblety was a woman-hater.

DR. FRANCIS TUMBLETY (1833-1903)

Dr. Francis Tumblety is another name regularly connected with Jack the Ripper. A letter written by Chief Inspector John George Littlechild to G.R. Sims on 23rd September 1913, points the finger of suspicion at Tumblety: "amongst the suspects, and to my mind a very likely one, was a Dr. T... He was an American quack named Tumblety and was at one time a frequent visitor to London and on these occasions constantly brought under the notice of the police, there being a large dossier concerning him at Scotland Yard."

Tumblety was arrested in London on 7th November 1888, not for any charges connected with the murder of Whitechapel prostitutes, but for eight counts of gross indecency against four men. The date of the arrest appears to rule him out as a suspect for the murder of Mary Jane Kelly. In any case, Tumblety was bailed on 16th November and he fled England to escape to the United States. There are reports that a British detective, Inspector Walter Andrews, was sent to America to investigate Tumblety, but the detective was in Toronto, Canada – and may, or may not, have gone to New York to follow any Ripper leads.

When Tumblety's name is mentioned in connection with the Whitechapel murders, his interest in medical specimens is cited. The Ripper removed the uterus of his second and fourth victims (Annie Chapman and Catherine Eddowes), and Tumblety is said to have collected preserved wombs (although there is no proof of this). Furthermore, there is no evidence that Francis Tumblety visited Whitechapel during his time in London. Although the Littlechild letter acknowledges that Tumblety's "feelings toward women were remarkable and bitter in the extreme," it also states that "he was not known as a sadist (which the murderer unquestionably was)".

WALTER RICHARD SICKERT
(1860-1942)

A name that crops up time and time again in Ripper investigations is Sickert. Born in Munich, Walter Richard Sickert was a pupil to artist James McNeill Whistler and was friends with Edgar Degas, before becoming the most important British impressionist painter. He has also been depicted as an informant, an accomplice, the writer of one or more of the letters from 'Jack the Ripper' and, of course, the infamous killer himself. This book will examine him in further detail in *The Final Solution* and *Case Closed?*

The story of Walter Sickert and fellow artist and associate Florence Pash was revealed by Jean Overton Fuller. Florence Pash had received many letters in her youth from Walter Sickert, which were edited by Jean's mother, Violet Overton Fuller. It appears that, years later, while working together on the letters, Florence Pash revealed to Violet and Jean Overton Fuller that she believed that Walter Sickert was the Ripper. Pash met Sickert in the 1880s and he painted her several times. She claimed that he had fathered an illegitimate son named Joseph and that he also hired a nanny – a shopgirl called Mary Kelly – who had arrived in London from Cardiff. According to Pash, Kelly stopped working for Sickert because the pay was irregular and she drifted into prostitution. Kelly then began to blackmail Sickert, who murdered her and her friends.

Pash also revealed to Violet Overton Fuller that Sickert had seen all of the Ripper victims *in situ*, which would only have been possible if he had been the killer. In addition, Pash maintained that Sickert had painted some of the victims and left clues in other works. For example, in one version of his most famous work *Ennui*, there is a painting of a gull on the wall (meant to be taken as a connection with Sir William Withey Gull).

The great British impressionist painter Walter Sickert is
implicated by some theories as a plausible Jack the Ripper.

The Reverend Charles Lutwidge Dodgson, better known as Lewis Carroll, was proposed as a suspect in the 1990s by Richard Wallace.

LEWIS CARROLL
(1832–1898)

In recent years in particular, the hunt for Jack the Ripper has thrown many unusual suspects into the mix – and perhaps none are more far-fetched than famous writer Lewis Carroll, author of *Alice's Adventures in Wonderland* and *Through the Looking-Glass.* The name Lewis Carroll was in fact a pseudonym of the Reverend Charles Lutwidge Dodgson, mathematics tutor at Christ Church, Oxford, from 1855 to 1881. Dodgson had many friendships with young girls and he also took "artistic" nude photographs of many underage females.

American child psychotherapist Richard Wallace researched Carroll extensively before writing *The Agony of Lewis Carroll* (1990), which convinced the author that Dodgson was a tormented, repressed paedophile. Wallace went on to write *Jack the Ripper: Light-Hearted Friend* six years later, which set forward the case to accuse Dodgson and his friend Thomas Vere Bayne of carrying out the series of horrific Whitechapel murders.

Wallace argued in his book that Dodgson's guilt was proved by anagrams in his own writings and how every Ripper murder was linked to the number 42. The significance of 42 is that Lewis Carroll frequently used the same number in the types of mathematical word and language games he loved in his books. Although Wallace uses anagrams from *Sylvie et Bruno* as "evidence", the book was written in 1887, predating the Ripper murders. Wallace's theories also fall down when Dodgson and Bayne's movements are examined during the 'Autumn of Terror': for some of the murder dates, neither of the men were close to London. Furthermore, Wallace failed to mention a meeting that took place between Dodgson and Dr. George Dabbs, a general practitioner in Shanklin, on the Isle of Wight. Dodgson had recorded in his journal for the date 26th August 1891 a discussion they had "about his very ingenious theory about Jack the Ripper".

DR. THOMAS JOHN BARNARDO (1845-1905)

Born in Dublin in 1845, Thomas John Barnardo preached in the city's slums at a young age. He moved to London, starting medical studies in 1866 at the London Hospital on Whitechapel Road. He saw the poverty of London's East End at first hand, and this led to his great work of philanthropy, setting up the charity that continues to bear his name today. He opened his first home for destitute boys in Stepney in 1870.

On 6th October 1888, at the height of the Jack the Ripper scare, Dr. Barnardo wrote a letter to *The Times* on the subject of children living in common lodging houses. His work took him out on the worst streets of the East End, and here he mentions the Ripper's third victim, Elizabeth Stride.

"Only four days before the recent murders I visited No.32 Flower and Dean Street, the house in which the unhappy woman Stride occasionally lodged. I had been examining many of the common lodging-houses in Bethnal Green that night... In the kitchen of No.32 there were... girls and women of the same unhappy class as that to which poor Elizabeth Stride belonged... The female inmates of the kitchen seemed thoroughly frightened at the dangers to which they were presumably exposed... One poor creature, who had evidently been drinking, exclaimed... 'We're all up to no good, and no one cares what becomes of us. Perhaps some of us will be killed next!'"

Dr. Barnardo claimed that he had later gone to the mortuary and seen the body of Stride and realised that she had been present on the night of his visit. The deputy of the lodging house of Elizabeth Stride denied that she had been in the kitchen that evening. Whether the doctor's story was true or not, it is difficult to reconcile the image of this compassionate philanthropist with a warped serial killer.

Dr. Barnardo was first recorded as a suspect in
a 1960s edition of *The Identity of Jack the Ripper*.

Well-to-do Liverpool merchant James Maybrick became associated with
the murders when the Maybrick Journal emerged in the 1990s.

JAMES MAYBRICK
(1838–1889)

James Maybrick, an upper-middle class cotton trader from Liverpool, became a Ripper suspect based on the discovery of a diary, known as the *Maybrick Journal*. Maybrick – a drug-taker – died as a result of arsenic poisoning, apparently murdered by his wife Florence. She was convicted for his murder, although it was noted that the judge Sir James Fitzjames Stephen was mentally unstable: after 15 years in jail, she was eventually released. In the vital document, Maybrick claimed that he was driven to murder prostitutes in 1888 by his wife's infidelity.

The *Maybrick Journal* itself is a Victorian scrapbook with 63 pages of handwritten text, with 48 pages at the beginning of the journal having been removed using a knife. The text begins mid-sentence and ends with the signature of Jack the Ripper: in between it documents what is supposed to be a written record of what the Ripper does from April 1888 to May 1889. James Maybrick writes that, having seen his wife with a lover in Whitechapel, Liverpool, he is so tormented by the infidelity that he is driven to murder a prostitute in Manchester, before continuing his vengeful trail of murders in Whitechapel in London.

The diary emerged suddenly in 1991, when Michael Barrett was given the journal by a drinking buddy, Tony Devereux, without any explanation apart from saying that it was genuine. Investigative author Shirley Harrison tells the tale of the journal's discovery and the controversy surrounding the find in *The Diary of Jack the Ripper* (2003). Many tests have been carried out on the Maybrick Journal, including ink analysis, but none has proved conclusive. Most handwriting experts believe that the journal was not written by the hand of James Maybrick. While most people believe that the Maybrick Journal is a forgery, they cannot agree whether it is a modern or old hoax.

AARON DAVIS COHEN
(1865-1889)

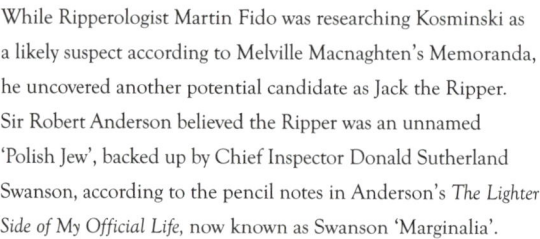

While Ripperologist Martin Fido was researching Kosminski as a likely suspect according to Melville Macnaghten's Memoranda, he uncovered another potential candidate as Jack the Ripper. Sir Robert Anderson believed the Ripper was an unnamed 'Polish Jew', backed up by Chief Inspector Donald Sutherland Swanson, according to the pencil notes in Anderson's *The Lighter Side of My Official Life*, now known as Swanson 'Marginalia'.

Fido found documentary evidence at Colney Hatch Asylum of "a young foreign Jew with dark brown hair, beard and eyes", who appeared before Thames Magistrates Court on 7th December 1888. He was named as Aaron Davis Cohen, or David Cohen. He was discharged from Whitechapel Workhouse Infirmary to Colney Hatch Asylum a fortnight later, on the 21st December. Part of his infirmary records include the following notes: "Suicidal Yes; Dangerous to Others Yes" and "Patient was brought in by police, who found him wandering at large and unable to take care of himself. Is supposed to have tried to commit suicide. Has been very violent since admission." Cohen died in Colney Hatch on 20th October 1889, with the cause of death recorded as "Exhaustion of Mania and Pulmonary Phthisis [tuberculosis or similar wasting disease]".

David Cohen fits the general profile given by Anderson and approved by Swanson, however vague that is. In addition, his incarceration in an asylum fits with the end of the "Canonical Five" murders. Although FBI profiler John Douglas had previously endorsed Aaron Kosminski as the most likely Ripper suspect (in 1988 for *The Secret Identity of Jack the Ripper*), when he reviewed the case in the light of the newly-found information about Cohen, he stated:

"I'm now prepared to say that Jack the Ripper was either the man known to the police as David Cohen... or someone very much like him."

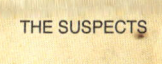

SKETCH OF THE MAN
WHO VISITED Mr LUSK

A frequent description of Jack the Ripper is dark-haired
with a Jewish appearance. The bearded Cohen fitted
the portrait of a killer: he was also violent and insane.

"Who is he? What is he? Where is he???" from *Puck* magazine in 1889. But is it possible that Jack the Ripper was a woman?

'JILL THE RIPPER'

Jill the Ripper? It may sound far-fetched, but perhaps a female killer is not quite as unlikely as it first appears. Lord Sidney Godolphin Osborne wrote a letter to *The Times* on 18th September 1888 in which he speculated that the wounds and mutilations carried out on the bodies of the Whitechapel murder victims were the physical manifestations of the type of threats that one prostitute might make to another. Perhaps he was an early example of someone espousing the importance of thinking outside the box. His letter stated, "it is within the range of my belief that one or both [Nichols/Chapman] these Whitechapel murders may have been committed by female hands. There are details in both cases which fit in well with language forever used where two of these unfortunates are in violent strife... There are, I have no doubt, plenty of women of this class known for their violent temper, with physical power to commit such a deed."

The strange notion of a female Ripper was also proposed by none other than Sir Arthur Conan Doyle, the creator of the legendary fictional detective Sherlock Holmes. He thought that the murderer could have been a woman, or even a man disguised as a female. William Stewart, author of *Jack the Ripper – A New Theory*, published in 1939, took the idea even further as he explored the possibility of a "Jill the Ripper". Conan Doyle had argued that a woman could move freely through the streets of Whitechapel, and even with a bloodstained apron, it would be assumed that she was a midwife. Stewart added to the theory, proposing that "Jill the Ripper" was an abortionist. In the 1970s, Detective Superintendent Arthur Butler picked up Stewart's theory, and based his own argument around the "fact" that Mary Jane Kelly was pregnant – although Dr. Bond's contemporary medical report demonstrated that she was not pregnant.

THE SEARCH CONTINUES

THE FINAL SOLUTION

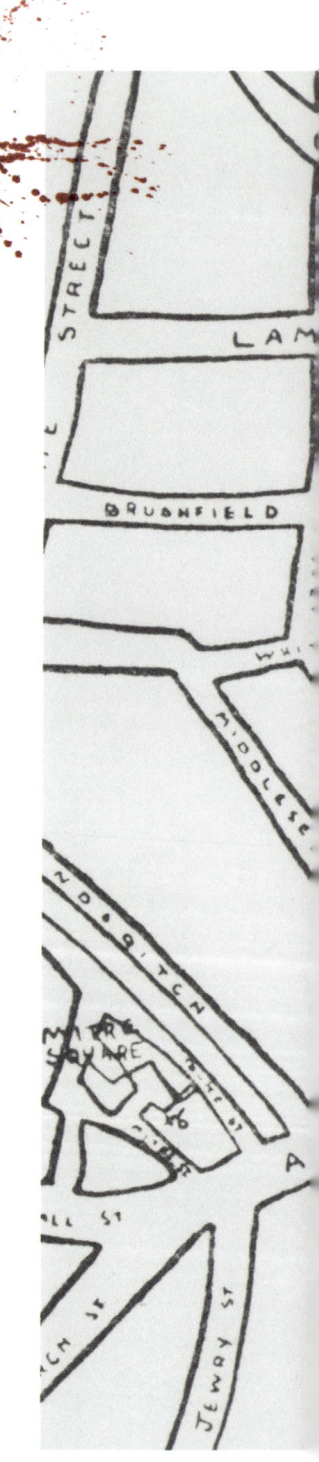

In 1976, Stephen Knight published *Jack the Ripper – The Final Solution*. The book was a bestseller, widely read and generally believed for over a decade. The new theory had a rather convoluted plot that involved Ripper victim Mary Jane Kelly, painter Walter Sickert, Prince Albert Victor, Sir William Withey Gull – and a cast of thousands of Freemasons. It was a Ripper conspiracy theory, and readers lapped it up.

Mary Jane Kelly, the fifth victim of the Ripper, witnesses the illegal marriage of Prince Albert Victor and Annie Elizabeth Crook, a Catholic. Kelly (and her prostitute friends) realises that this – especially the Catholic part – would rock the nation and the Freemasons. She decides to blackmail the government, and Prime Minister Salisbury enlists the aid of Queen's surgeon Sir William Withey Gull to shut her and her acquaintances up. There is not one Ripper, but three – Gull, Sickert and a mysterious coachman named Netley. Together they rip up the blackmailing prostitutes. That's the story.

This ripping yarn was handed to Knight by Joseph Sickert, who claimed to be a relative of painter Walter Sickert, implicated in this version of Ripper events. The conspiracy involved the Freemasons, with great emphasis placed on Masonic rituals and how the Ripper corpses were mutilated. However, none of the mutilations had any link to the history of real Freemason rituals. Knight's story states that the victims were killed elsewhere then taken to the various murder sites. Contemporary doctors did wonder about this theory, and then dismissed the possibility because the blood evidence suggests they were killed where they were found. There are many other inaccuracies and all sorts of omissions in this entertaining, illusory tale – many Ripper experts have pointed out that there is not a scrap of historical evidence to support these outlandish claims. In 1978, Joseph Sickert himself denounced the Jack the Ripper part of the tale saying, "It was a hoax; I made it all up... a whopping fib."

Stephen Knight published a well-known conspiracy theory as a solution to
the Jack the Ripper murders. One of the murderers was eminent surgeon Sir
William Withey Gull (above).

The gruesome mystery of Jack the Ripper captured imaginations all over the world, this illustration featured in a French magazine in 1909.

A FRESH SUSPECT

Born in 1865, Timothy Donovan was the deputy manager of a common lodging-house establishment known as Crossingham's, at 35 Dorset Street, where the second Ripper victim Annie Chapman lived. Donovan was described as "a thin, pale-faced, sullen-looking young man, with a... closely twisted crimson scarf around his throat". Donovan divulged to the press that he knew the so-called Leather Apron, and that he had thrown him out of the lodging house when he assaulted a woman. As the *Evening Standard* reported on 10th September 1888, Donovan continued to refuse Leather Apron entry at the door of the lodging house.

As the keeper of Crossingham's, Donovan stated that he had known Annie Chapman for about 16 months before her death, although she had only lodged at the house for about four months. He saw her on 8th September 1888 at about 1.45 am, eating a baked potato in the kitchen of the lodging house, not long before she was murdered.

In *The Complete Jack the Ripper* published in 2004, Ripper expert Donald Rumbelow proposed a plausible theory that Timothy Donovan could have been Jack the Ripper. As keeper of Crossingham's, he would not have aroused suspicion in the prostitutes if he were to approach them. As well as being familiar with Annie Chapman, it is likely that he knew both Catherine Eddowes and Mary Jane Kelly. Furthermore, if Timothy Donovan was the Ripper, he might well have elaborated his story about Leather Apron to divert any attention away from himself. Author Donald Rumbelow further identified Donovan as a 29-year-old-man from St George's-in-the-East, who died on 1st November 1888, due to cirrhosis of the liver, phthisis and exhaustion. However, Mary Jane Kelly died just over a week later, so if Donovan was Jack the Ripper, then another killer would have to be responsible for Kelly's murder.

CASE CLOSED?

Patricia Cornwell is a popular crime writer, famous for her series of novels featuring medical examiner Kay Scarpetta, including *Postmortem* and *Body of Evidence*. Her fiction books sell by the million. In 2002, Cornwell wrote *Portrait of a Killer: Jack the Ripper – Case Closed*, a non-fiction book, where Cornwell set out to prove that painter Walter Sickert – once again – was Jack the Ripper.

Her book argued that Sickert suffered from a fistula (abnormal opening) of the penis and needed operations as a child to correct the condition, leaving him impotent. However, Sickert's first marriage to Ellen Cobden was thought to be unhappy due to his adultery. The painter was married twice more and believed to have fathered at least one illegitimate child. Furthermore, in 1865 Sickert attended St Mark's Hospital in City Road – a specialist colorectal centre (for treatment of fistula of the rectum, not genitalia).

Cornwell contends that many of Sickert's paintings show similarities to post-mortem Ripper photographs. Sickert was perhaps fascinated by the Ripper case, but that does not make him the killer. Respected British art historian Richard Shone summed up his dismay at Cornwell's flawed arguments; "She draws upon assumptions, plays fast and loose with facts, misinterprets language and makes fanciful readings of Sickert's paintings... She quotes evidence to support her view but ignores it when it doesn't suit her case."

Cornwell tried to use modern forensic techniques, but her starting point was flawed. She wanted to prove, through testing, that Sickert's letters matched DNA found on Ripper letters (thought to be hoaxes by most Ripper experts). Although the Dr. Openshaw letter potentially matched one from Sickert, it was an imprecise mitochondrial-DNA test – so in 1888, it could have come from any one of 40,000 people living in London. Cornwell had spent six million dollars, but proved nothing. Perhaps Patricia Cornwell could have saved herself the expense and withering criticism she received if she had first considered that, during September 1888, it appeared that Sickert was on holiday in France.

Walter Sickert painted many bedroom interiors, including *The Camden Town Murder or What Shall We Do about the Rent?*. The titles for his paintings were often deliberately confusing or playful.

AUTOBIOGRAPHY OF JACK THE RIPPER

Written in the 1920s, discovered in 2008, and published in 2011, *The Autobiography of Jack the Ripper* is a recent, unique addition to the many volumes on the subject of Whitechapel's legendary killer. Ripper expert Paul Begg introduces the book, stating, "This book is the autobiography of a man who claims that for a few short weeks when he was a young man he killed several women in Whitechapel. This book claims to be the autobiography of Jack the Ripper. The alleged author is James Willoughby Carnac, a man whose name is otherwise unknown, who is untraceable, and who may not have existed. This autobiography looks like a work of fiction. But things are never that simple."

Will we ever know the true identity of the cold-blooded killer who prowled the streets and alleyways of Whitechapel in the autumn of 1888?

In this autobiographical account, Carnac recounts his early
life in Part one, up to 1888. Part two of the book concerns
the extraordinary events of 1888, when the author is supposed
to be about 28 years of age. Including the epilogue, Part three
is written in a different style and is "a very contrived, very poor
fiction" according to the analysis of Paul Begg. Carnac describes
his young adult years in London and sheds some light on what
made him murder poor "unfortunates" in Whitechapel during
the autumn of 1888. However, it is noticeable that Carnac
displays a true lack of motive in slitting the throats of his victims
and disembowelling a number of them: he is simply driven
to carry out such barbaric acts. He then states what happened
in a very cold manner to the reader.

Is *The Autobiography of Jack the Ripper* a true confession
from "Saucy Jacky"? Does it ring true? Or is this merely an
interesting piece of period writing? Most experts believe
it is a fake, dating from the 1920s, but if so, it also is a
fascinating, well-researched hoax.

Now, as it was then at the time of Jack the Ripper, Christ Church
continues to tower above the nearby streets of Spitalfields.

ON THE RIPPER'S TRAIL... IN LONDON TODAY

More than 125 years later, Jack the Ripper continues to captivate us: the brutal murders, the mystery of his identity... and the atmospheric setting of Victorian London. For those with an interest in true crimes, the vicarious need to follow the footsteps of a real-life killer can be hard to resist: and there are many walking tours after-dark in the East End that can enhance our imaginative leap into the past.

Much of the Ripper's London has disappeared, especially the actual murder sites, but there are relics from the past, where we can piece together some of the history. On the corner of Fournier Street, along the busy thoroughfare of Commercial Street, stands the Ten Bells public house, which some reports connected with Annie Chapman and Mary Kelly. All the victims were alcoholics so it is possible that they had all drunk there in the past. Opposite the pub is the imposing white structure of Christ Church, Spitalfields.

Buck's Row, the site of the first Ripper murder, has disappeared, at least, on a map. Look for its new name, Durward Street, and you can find a car park where the murder happened. The Boarding School still dominates the street, as it did in 1888, but it is now known as Trinity Hall flats. A car park now also occupies the site of Dorset Street, where Mary Kelly was murdered. Berner Street, where Elizabeth Stride was killed, is now Henriques Street and Dutfield's Yard is replaced with a school playground. Mitre Square still exists, but it is surrounded by modern buildings. If we are looking for atmosphere and authenticity, perhaps the best place to head for is the White Hart on Whitechapel High Street at night. Right next to the pub is an arched, cobbled passageway leading to George Yard (now called Gunthorpe Street). Further down on the left was George Yard Buildings, where in 1888 Martha Tabram was stabbed 39 times.

VICTIM'S NAME	DATE/TIME DISCOVERED	CRIME SCENE LOCATION
Mary Ann Nichols	Friday 31st Aug. 1888 (3.40 am)	Buck's Row (Durward Street today)
Annie Chapman	Saturday 8th Sept. 1888 (6.00 am)	29 Hanbury Street (backyard)
Elizabeth Stride	Sunday 30th Sept. 1888 (1.00 am)	Dutfield's Yard, off Berner Street (Henriques Street today)
Catherine Eddowes	Sunday 30th Sept. 1888 (1.45 am)	Mitre Square
Mary Jane Kelly	Friday 9th Nov. 1888 (10.45 am)	13 Miller's Court, off Dorset Street

CAUSE OF DEATH	MUTILATIONS
Haemorrhage (severing of both common carotid arteries)	Disembowelment
Strangled/suffocated then throat severed (haemorrhage)	Uterus removed/missing
Haemorrhage (partial severing of left common carotid artery)	None
Haemorrhage (severing of left common carotid artery)	Uterus and left kidney removed/missing, cuts to face, mutilations to abdomen
Haemorrhage (severing of right common carotid artery)	Disembowelment, severe mutilations, heart removed/missing, face gashed

TIMELINE

1888

3rd April: Emma Elizabeth Smith attacked in Brick Lane. Dies later in the London Hospital, Whitechapel Road.

July: Suspect Michael Ostrog arrested for theft in Paris, France and held in custody (until November 1888). Suspect Robert Donston Stephenson enters the London Hospital as a private patient.

7th August: Martha Tabram murdered in George Yard Buildings, George Yard.
31st August: Mary Ann Nichols, the Ripper's first certain victim, murdered in Buck's Row.

September: Suspect Walter Sickert thought to be on holiday in France.
1st September: Sir Robert Anderson appointed Assistant Commissioner of the Metropolitan CID. Chief Inspector Donald Swanson is put in charge of the Whitechapel murder investigation by Sir Charles Warren (until 6th October).
7th September: Police report identifies suspect Leather Apron as John Pizer.
8th September: Annie Chapman, the Ripper's second victim, murdered at 29 Hanbury Street. Sir Robert Anderson begins his sick leave, travelling to Switzerland.
10th September: Sergeant William Thick arrests 'Leather Apron' suspect, John Pizer.
12th September: Sidney Godolphin Osborne's letter about Whitechapel's "warren of foul alleys" to *The Times* is published.
17th September: Ripper letter dated "17th September 1888" found in the National Archives (a century later in 1988).
18th September: Sidney Godolphin Osborne writes letter to *The Times* suggesting that Jack the Ripper could be a woman.
27th September: "Dear Boss" letter received at *Central News Agency*. Signed "Jack the Ripper".

29th September: "Dear Boss" letter forwarded to
Metropolitan Police.

30th September: The double murder – Elizabeth Stride,
the Ripper's third victim, murdered at Dutfield's Yard, and
Catherine Eddowes, the Ripper's fourth victim, murdered
in Mitre Square. Goulston Street graffito discovered.

October: Michael Ostrog, according to Police Gazette wanted for
failure to report to the police.

1st October: "Saucy Jacky" postcard sent to *Central News Agency*.

6th October: Dr. Thomas John Barnardo writes a letter to
The Times about children in lodging houses, mentioning
Elizabeth Stride.

16th October: George Akin Lusk receives the letter "From
Hell" – and half a kidney – in the post. Suspect Robert Donston
Stephenson writes to the police, suggesting that Dr. Morgan
Davies is the Ripper.

29th October: A Jack the Ripper letter is sent to Dr. Openshaw.

1st November: Timothy Donovan dies (suspect proposed by
Donald Rumbelow).

7th November: Dr. Francis Tumblety arrested in London
on a number of charges against four men.

8th November: Sir Charles Warren's resignation is accepted.

9th November: Mary Jane Kelly, the Ripper's fifth victim,
murdered at 13 Miller's Court, Dorset Street.

10th November: Dr. Thomas Bond prepares a profile of Jack the
Ripper after carrying out post-mortem on Mary Jane Kelly.

12th November: George Hutchinson makes statement to
police about Mary Jane Kelly meeting a stranger (from 2.00 am
onwards on the 9th November).

30th November: Montague John Druitt dismissed as a teacher
from Blackheath boarding school for "serious trouble".

7th December: Robert Donston Stephenson leaves the London Hospital. David Cohen appears before Thames Magistrates Court.

21st December: David Cohen sent to Colney Hatch Asylum.

31st December: Body of Montague John Druitt found in the River Thames.

1889

17th July: Alice McKenzie (or "Claypipe Annie") murdered in Castle Alley.

10th September: Unidentified female torso found in Pinchin Street.

20th October: David Cohen dies in Colney Hatch Asylum.

1890

January: Suspect Sir William Withey Gull dies.

1891

13th February: Frances Coles murdered in Swallow Gardens.

April: Thomas Cutbush sent to Broadmoor Criminal Lunatic Asylum.

26th August: Lewis Carroll notes in his journal a discussion with Dr. George Dabbs "ingenious theory about Jack the Ripper". Prince Albert Victor Christian Edward (Prince Eddy) becomes Duke of Clarence and Avondale.

1894

13th February: *The Sun* begins to publish a series of articles proposing Thomas Cutbush (although he is not named) as Jack the Ripper.

23rd February: Sir Melville Macnaghten refutes claims by *The Sun* regarding Cutbush by writing *Macnaghten memoranda*.

1910

Sir Robert Anderson's memoirs *The Lighter Side of My Official Life* are published.

1913

23rd September: John George Littlechild writes to G.R. Sims suggesting Dr. Francis Tumblety as a suspect.

1919

Aaron Kosminski dies in Leavesden Asylum, near Watford.

1939

William Stewart publishes *Jack the Ripper – A New Theory*, exploring the idea that Jack the Ripper was a female abortionist.

1962

Philippe Jullian publishes his *Edouard VII*, suggesting the name of Prince Eddy as Jack the Ripper.

1970

Dr. Thomas Stowell identifies Prince Eddy (as the disguised "Mr. S") in his article *Jack the Ripper – A Solution?* in the *Criminologist*.

1976

Stephen Knight's account of Masonic intrigue *Jack the Ripper: The Final Solution* is published.

1978

Joseph Sickert confesses that the Jack the Ripper part of Knight's *Jack the Ripper: The Final Solution* was "a whopping fib".

1987

Swanson marginalia (by Chief Inspector Donald Sutherland Swanson) is published.

1988

Modern psychological profile of Jack the Ripper on television documentary *The Secret Identity of Jack the Ripper* created by John Douglas and Roy Hazelwood. Ripper letter dated 17th September 1888 found in National Archives by Peter McClelland.

1991

The Maybrick Journal, the diary of James Maybrick during the Ripper murders, emerges.

1996

Richard Wallace publishes *Jack the Ripper: Light-Hearted Friend* accusing Lewis Carroll and Thomas Vere Bayne of carrying out the murders.

Picture Credits:
4–5 Mary Evans Picture Library; 6 George Peters/Getty Images; 7 lynea/Shutterstock; 8–9 Print Collector/Getty Images; 10–11 Culture Club/Getty Images; 12–13 Charles Booth/University of Michigan; 13 Mansell/Time & Life Pictures/Getty Images; 14–15 Getty Images; 16–17 Mary Evans Picture Library/Epic; 18–19 The Bridgeman Art Library/Getty Images; 20 PVDE/Epic/Mary Evans; 22 The Bridgeman Art Library/Getty Images; 24–25 The British Library/Robana; 26–27 The British Library/Robana; 28–29 Mary Evans Picture Library; 30–31 Mary Evans Picture Library/DAVID LEWIS HODGSON; 32 PVDE/Epic/Mary Evans; 35 Guildhall Library & Art Gallery/Heritage Images/Getty Images; 36–37 British Library/Robana via Getty Images; 38–39 British Library/Robana via Getty Images; 40–41 Mary Evans Picture Library; 43 Mary Evans Picture Library; 44 PVDE/Epic/Mary Evans; 47 British Library/Robana via Getty Images; 48–49 The Bridgeman Art Library/Getty Images; 50–51 The Bridgeman Art Library/Getty Images; 52–53 The Bridgeman Art Library/Getty Images; 54 British Library/Robana via Getty Images; 56–57 Mary Evans Picture Library/DAVID LEWIS HODGSON; 58 Mary Evans Picture Library/DAVID LEWIS HODGSON; 61 Mary Evans Picture Library; 63 Mary Evans Picture Library; 64 Mary Evans Picture Library/DAVID LEWIS HODGSON; 66–67 The British Library/Robana; 69 The British Library/Robana; 70–71 Mary Evans/Epic/Tallandier; 72–73 Mary Evans/Peter Higginbotham Collection; 74–75 The Bridgeman Art Library/Getty Images; 76–77 Universal History Archive/UIG via Getty Images; 78–79 INTERFOTO/Sammlung Rauch/Mary Evans; 80 Mary Evans Picture Library; 82–83 Mary Evans Picture Library; 84 Mary Evans Picture Library; 86–87 The British Library/Robana via Getty Images; 88 Tal/Epic/Mary Evans; 90–91 Mary Evans Picture Library; 93 Mary Evans Picture Library/TOM MORGAN; 94–95 The British Library/Robana via Getty Images; 97 Mary Evans/The National Archives, London. England; 98–99 Will Rose-Pool/Getty Images; 100–101 Juergen Vollmer/Redferns/Getty Images; 102t Illustrated London News Ltd/Mary Evans; 102bl Mary Evans Picture Library/DAVID LEWIS HODGSON; 102br Unknown/Wikimedia Commons; 105 Mary Evans Picture Library; 106–107 Bentley Archive/Popperfoto/Getty Images; 108–109 CARL DE SOUZA/AFP/Getty Images; 110 Mary Evans Picture Library; 112–113 Mary Evans Picture Library/DAVID LEWIS HODGSON; 115 Hulton Archive/Stringer/Getty Images; 116–117 Illustrated London News Ltd/Mary Evans; 118–199 Keystone/Stringer/Getty Images; 120–121 De Agostini/Getty Images; 122–123 Illustrated London News Ltd/Mary Evans; 125 INTERFOTO/Sammlung Rauch/Mary Evans; 125b Original uploader was Jack1956/Wikimedia Commons; 126 Mary Evans Picture Library; 129 Mary Evans Picture Library/DAVID LEWIS HODGSON; 130 Illustrated London News Ltd/Mary Evans; 133t Illustrated London News Ltd/Mary Evans; 133m Unknown/Wikimedia Commons; 133b Mary Evans Picture Library/DONALD RUMBELOW; 134 Unknown/Wikimedia Commons; 137 Mary Evans Picture Library; 138 Illustrated London News Ltd/Mary Evans; 141 Unknown/Wikimedia Commons; 142 Unknown/Wikimedia Commons; 145 George C. Beresford/Beresford/Getty Images; 146 Mansell/Time Life Pictures/Getty Images; 149 Universal History Archive/Getty Images; 150 Mary Evans/Epic/PVDE; 153 Popperfoto/Getty Images; 154 The British Library/Robana via Getty Images; 156–157 Fragles/Dreamstime; 158–159 b/g Hulton Archive/Getty Images; 159t Hulton Archive/Getty Images; 160 Mary Evans Picture Library/Epic; 162–163 Walter Sickert/Wikimedia Commons; 164–165 Carlos Lopez-Barillas/Getty Images; 166 Arcaid/UIG via Getty Images.
Ends: Mary Evans Picture Library/Epic; Charles Booth/University of Michigan; De Agostini/Getty Images; Mary Evans Picture Library

2002

Patricia Cornwell publishes *Portrait of a Killer: Jack the Ripper – Case Closed*.

2003

Shirley Harrison publishes *The Diary of Jack the Ripper* about the Maybrick Journal.

2004

Donald Rumbelow proposes Timothy Donovan as a plausible Ripper suspect in *The Complete Jack the Ripper*.

2008

The *Autobiography of Jack the Ripper* by James Willoughby Carnac is discovered.

2011

James Willoughby Carnac's *Autobiography of Jack the Ripper* is published.